"ENGLISH TINGLAZED TILES"
by
JONATHAN HORNE

A painted wooden panel intended for sealing a fireplace when not in use.
English, circa 1730.

ACKNOWLEDGEMENTS

I would like to thank the following institutions and private collectors who have kindly allowed their pieces to be illustrated in this Catalogue:
Mr. and Mrs. Michael Baron, Christopher Birkett, Birmingham Museum & Art Gallery, Frank Britton, Christie's, City of Bristol Museum & Art Gallery, Henry Duke & Son, Glasgow Museums & Art Galleries, Guildford Museum, Hampshire County Museum Service, Trevor Micklem, The Museum of London, National Museums & Galleries on Merseyside, Arnold Page, People's Palace Museum Glasgow, The Reverend and Mrs. G. Prime, Anthony Ray, Alistair Sampson, Chris Sheffield, Mr. and Mrs. Graham Slater, Sotheby's, Surrey Archaeological Society, Fred Vogel and Roger Warner.

I am sincerely grateful to the following who have helped and advised with the production of this book:
Mr. M. J. Alexander, Michael Archer, Kate Arnold-Foster, Lionel Burman, Myra Brown, John Cox, E. Derkssen-Weeda, M. Donnelly, Barbara Drew, Gillian Everard, The Reverend H. Huggill, Jonathan Kinghorn, Hans Van Lemmen, Margaret MacFarlane, Arnold Page, The Reverend G. Prime, Mr. J. Pluis, Anthony Ray, Mr. and Mrs. Graham Slater, Karin Walton and Rosemary Weinstein.
Particular mention must go to Hazel Forsyth from the Museum of London and also David Drakard for his information on tile printing. I am most grateful to Anna Sanderson for her assistance and who has also undertaken all the drawings and typing.

© Jonathan Horne 1989
First published in 1989 by
Jonathan Horne
66c Kensington Church Street
London, W8 4BY

ISBN 0 9512140 2 0

Designed by Jonathan Horne

Printed in Great Britain by
Grillford Ltd., Granby, Milton Keynes

CONTENTS

The Making of Tiles	4
Tile Production in the British Isles	5
Identification	9
"Paving Tyles"	13
Seventeenth Century Wall Tiles	17
Eighteenth Century Wall Tiles	
—European Figures and Landscapes	19
—Animals	48
—Birds	54
—Chinoiserie	56
—Flowers	60
—Stylized Flowers and Patterns	71
Biblical Subjects—Old Testament	75
—New Testament	95
Recess Tiles	110
Tile Pictures	114
Transfer Printed Tiles	124
Bibliography	135

INTRODUCTION

In 1973 Anthony Ray produced his excellent book, "English Delftware Tiles" (Faber and Faber Ltd). This has remained the authoritative work on the subject for collectors and connoisseurs but unfortunately has been out of print for some time. Over the last ten years I have gathered together a large number of tiles which include many formerly in the Lipski and Hodgkin Collections. It seemed the opportunity should not be missed to publish this unique group before they became dispersed. Subsequently with the addition of generous loans from private sources and Museums, this catalogue has been produced.

Where appropriate the listings have been cross-referenced to Ray's book and with new information and many previously unrecorded tiles it is hoped that this Catalogue will serve as a useful reference work for the further identification of 'English Tinglazed Tiles'.

J.K.H.

Those book that have been constantly referred to throughout the text have been listed in brackets as follows:
(Britton) "London Delftware"—Frank Britton (Jonathan Horne 1987)
(Horne) "A Catalogue of English Delftware Tiles"—Jonathan Horne (Jonathan Horne 1980)
(Hume) "Early English Delftware from London and Virginia"—Ivor Noël Hume (Colonial Williamsburg Occasional
    Papers in Archaeology, Volume II, Colonial Williamsburg Foundation 1977)
(Lipski) "Dated English Delftware"—L. Lipski & M. Archer (Sotheby Publications 1984)
(Ray) "English Delftware Tiles"—Anthony Ray (Faber & Faber 1973).

THE MAKING OF TILES

PREPARATION:
Clays of different types were blended together to get the right consistency; a difficult task with which the London potters had problems during the late 17th and early 18th centuries. The clay would be rolled out like pastry, roughly cut up into squares and placed into wooden or iron frames. After being partly dried the tiles were again rolled to obtain a flat surface and re-cut with the aid of a square board before being dried further. Sometimes the board had a copper pin at each corner (or on diagonally opposite corners) which helped the cutter manoeuvre and grip the tile. This method left holes in the corners of the tiles and was not favoured by all the manufacturers. The edges were trimmed, either vertically or were slightly undercut whilst the tiles were still in a leather state. (The size and thickness of these tiles varied considerably, although the average size is approximately 12.7 sq. x 0.7 cms.). The tiles were then fired for the first time at 1800° F which resulted in a "biscuit" tile ready for glazing.

DECORATION:
A liquid tin glaze was applied to one side of the biscuit tile, very soon through evaporation and the absorbent nature of the clay, the glaze became a thin white powder-like substance. The tiles were now ready for the decorator and great care had to be taken not to knock or touch the surface of the glaze, as until it was fired it was very friable.
The painter copied his designs from a variety of sources; books, prints and in many cases directly from Dutch tiles. The outline of these patterns were usually copied with the help of a stencil. This was a square piece of paper with the design pricked out and was placed over the glazed tile before fine charcoal was pounced through the little holes. On removing the paper the faint design was ready for the decorator to "fill in". Often the same subject was used but with different borders, (p. 10, nos. **A & B**), and with different backgrounds (p. 10, nos. **E & F**), which perhaps indicates the use of more than one stencil. Sometimes the subject was shown in reverse (cf. nos. **454-455**), which means the stencil was used the other way round. Most of the decorating was done in blue although manganese was popular and polychrome was also used. After painting the tiles would be fired for the second time at 1800° F during which the tin glaze fused with the pigments and took on its familiar appearance.
A document in the Manchester Public Library (Ray, p. 37) lists:

Fine painted Tyles and white Tyles		
Large, the Foot being 4 Tyles	at 16d.	pr Foot
Fine painted small	7d.	do.
Ditto—a 2 sort of painted	4d.	do.
Ditto—y worst painted	2d	do.
Large. Fine white tyles	8d.	do.
Ditto—small. The best	4d.	do.
Ditto—ordinary white	2d.	do.

It is interesting to note that decorated tiles were almost twice the price of plain. There was also a ready demand for seconds and even thirds. Those tiles that did not reach these categories were often used in the kiln as supports.

TILE PRODUCTION IN THE BRITISH ISLES

LONDON

During the second half of the 16th century Protestant craftsmen in Antwerp were fleeing the religious persecution of the Spanish Inquisition. Several potters came to England and in 1567 a factory was briefly established in Norwich producing "Galleyware" (tin-glazed earthenware) and "Gally paving tyles". These facts are revealed in the famous 1570 petition of Jasper Andries and Jacob Jansen to Queen Elizabeth in which they request a twenty year patent with sole rights of manufacture in England (Britton, p. 20).

Although this patent was not granted Jacob Jansen moved to the City of London in 1571 and worked at Aldgate with other Flemish potters. The wares they produced were almost identical to those made in Antwerp, and therefore positive identification of English types is very difficult.

During the early 17th century a number of factories were established south of the River Thames in Southwark. Christian Wilhelm's Pickleherring Quay factory is known to have produced "paving tyles" (Ray, p. 34) and some wasters were found during redevelopment of the site (Hume, p. 19). Recent excavations at Rotherhithe have recovered tile fragments amongst the kiln waste. "Paving tyles" have been found on many domestic sites in and around the metropolis and the Museum of London has an interesting collection (Britton, pp. 170-175). The similarity of English and Dutch tiles at this time was very close but by the mid 17th century fashions changed and the production of "paving tyles" ceased.

In Holland during the second half of the 17th century it became popular to cover internal walls from floor to ceiling with tinglazed tiles and consequently vast amounts were produced. In England the use of tiles was usually limited to wash basin surrounds and fireplaces, and therefore the same quantities were never required.

Due to a lack of tile production in England during the latter part of the 17th century requirements were being met from Holland, but in 1676 a potter from Delft, Jan Ariens Van Hamme, set up a factory at Copthall, Lambeth and obtained a patent "to exercise his Art of Makeing Tiles and Porcelane and other earthenwares after the way practised in Holland". It seems unlikely that he made much impression on the industry, although it is possible that his factory produced the "Popish Plot" tiles (no. **12**). He died in 1680 and the London potters continued to have problems with the manufacture of tiles (Ray, p. 35).

Nathaniel Oade was the owner of the Gravel Lane pottery in Southwark, and it was written in 1718 that despite "Gally tiles for chimneys, being a very beneficial part of the Trade...", as there was "... not a Man in the Kingdom to be got, that could make them to any purpose, his son Thomas proposed to go to Holland and thence to bring a Person well skilled in that Art... his Father knew of his going and was glad of the Man's being brought over, which appeared by his readinesss to Article him, and by lending him a considerable sum to stay with him for Six Years". (Thomas Oade "A Full Reply" 1718).

When Nathaniel Oade died in 1726 an inventory of his estate was made, which listed every item in every room of the Gravel Lane pottery (Britton, p. 190). 79,411 items of delftware and 12,886 tiles are recorded as being held in stock. This list was made at one moment, in one year, at one factory. It makes one realise the enormous quantities that were produced and therefore what has survived today can only be a minute part of that production.*

During the 18th century large quantities of tiles were made at several London potteries. The William Griffith factory at Lambeth High Street displayed a large tile panel over their door inscribed "GRIFFITH 1751" (Britton, colour Pl. T) and fragments of a variety of tiles were recovered by Garner from building sites in the vicinity of this pottery (Ray, fig. 22-27). Pieces of tile have more recently been found at the Vauxhall site during excavations and road widening (E.C.C. Vol. 9, Part 2, 1974; and E.C.C. Vol. 12, Part 1, 1984). It is evident from comparing the styles of painting on the later tiles (pp. 30 and 38) that production continued in London certainly to the end of the 18th century.

---

*Note: It would appear that during the first half of the 18th century, London was by far the biggest producer of tinglazed wares with Bristol in third place, some way behind Liverpool. This conclusion has been drawn from the study of these tiles. The theory is also supported by the collection of 400 pieces of delftware at Colonial Williamsburg, which is at present being catalogued for future publication.

BRISTOL

Delftware was first made in the West Country at Brislington, a village just outside Bristol. This factory was first started around 1640 but it was not until 1683 that delftware began to be made in Bristol. There is no evidence to suppose that tiles were produced in Bristol itself until after 1720. Excavations at the Limekiln Lane potteries revealed many manganese powdered ground tiles and biblical subjects that were made until 1746 when the factory closed (Ray, p. 40). It is known that in 1750 the Redcliff Back pottery was also producing "Flemish tiles for grates" which is mentioned in the Edkins manuscript ("English Delftware Pottery"—Ray, pp. 64-65).

It is very probable that the tiles painted with the typical Bristol landscape scenes (p. 34) were produced here certainly until the end of the 1760's. Other tiles that can be related by quality and size include those with Bianco borders (p. 59) and the polychrome birds (p. 54). It is not known how long after 1770 tiles were being produced at Bristol.

WINCANTON

Tiles were manufactured at Wincanton in Somerset, a factory that was started in the 1730's and lasted for about 20 years. Fragments of parti-coloured tiles (no. **430**) were recovered from the pottery site during excavation and a similar tile in the Birmingham City Art Gallery is recorded as having come from the house of Nathaniel Ireson, who was the owner of the pottery. Other designs may have been made but if so, these have not yet been recognised. There was a large quantity of powdered manganese ware found amongst the waster fragments but these and the other finds closely resemble the Bristol types.

LIVERPOOL

The earliest reference to delftware being made in Liverpool comes from the "London Postboy" dated 23rd May 1710, and in which "tiles" are mentioned. Unfortunately little is known of this early period or how prolific production was. The first workmen were brought from Southwark therefore pieces made at this time would look distinctly London.

During the second half of the 18th century Liverpool tile production developed dramatically with the introduction of a range of exciting new designs and technical achievements, such as printing (p. 124). At this time they were producing a range of designs that were superior to anything being made in Holland.

There is documentary evidence that tiles were being made at the Old Haymarket pottery around 1765-70, and it is known that John Sadler was being supplied from this source with large quantities of blanks for his transfer printing (p. 124). Some of the later painted tiles have a very white glaze similar to the Dutch and have the appearance of being 19th century! (cf. no. **202**). It therefore seems likely that production continued to the end of the 18th century and perhaps later.

GLASGOW

In 1748 the Delftfield pottery was founded in Glasgow by a consortium of businessmen. Their first manager was John Bird from Lambeth who had probably served his apprenticeship under his uncle, Joseph Fortee, who was a partner at Barston's Port House in Lambeth (Griffiths), working his apprenticeship and clerking until his uncle's death in 1747 ("English Delftware"—Garner/Archer, p. 48-51).

Tiles were made at the Delftfield factory from the very start. It is known that Bird, who was only with the company for a couple of years, instructed one of his workmen in the making of tiles, ("Delftfield", p. 13) and the very first firing of the kiln (which collapsed) contained some 200 tiles ("Delftfield", p. 34). The company advertised in the "Glasgow Courant" in 1752, 1757 and 1760, and their wares included "chimney tiles". Trade was very successful and thousands of pieces of delftware were exported annually but no Delftfield tiles have been positively identified, although "biscuit" tiles (13 x 0.8 cms) were found during excavation of the pottery.

An interesting set of 24 blue and powdered manganese tiles exists in the Red Bedroom at Pollok House, Glasgow (fig. I). These are unlike any Dutch tile and have more in common with the powdered London tiles of the 1740's and 50's. However the style of painting is quite different with deeper manganese borders and the "Daisy" corner motif is unrecorded. There is therefore, a strong possibility that these are from the Delftfield pottery, a theory supported by the recovery of a single tile (no. **24**) of the same type which was found in 1977 in the grounds of Glenarbuck House, the 18th century home of Provost Gilbert Hamilton of Glasgow who was one of the chief partners in the Delftfield Company. Several other tiles were also recovered from this source, most of which were of typical Liverpool designs (bird in blue, manganese chinoiserie figures, buttercup corner), but one of these is distinctly different being decorated in manganese with an unusual pattern that is unrecorded on English tiles (no. **421**).

IRELAND

There is no documentary evidence to say that delftware tiles were made in Ireland. If they were made they would have the appearance of the Liverpool types and may well lie unrecognised within this catalogue (pp. 66-67).

Fig. I. Part of a fireplace surround in the Red Bedroom at Pollok House, Glasgow. (Reproduced by kind permission of Glasgow Museums and Art Galleries).

The fireplace contains 24 tiles altogether and those not shown are repeats of the ones illustrated. The tiles (12.8 cms square) are decorated in blue with powdered manganese, and may have been made at the Delftfield factory, Glasgow, being unlike any other English tile (compare with the more typical powdered tiles on pp. 19-25). Another tile of this type was recovered from the grounds of Glenarbuck House, Glasgow (cf. no. **24**).

IDENTIFICATION

It is known that delftware tiles were made in London, Bristol, Wincanton, Liverpool, Glasgow and very possibly at other centres that have not been identified. Unfortunately archaeological evidence is almost non-existent due to the lack of tile wasters from sites since there was always a market for seconds and even thirds. Only a handful of unstratified shards have been recovered from various locations and one has to rely on styles of painting, thickness, colour, size, etc. Some groups are more obvious than others, which has resulted in a basic breakdown of tiles into factory types although a certain degree of uncertainty must remain on some of these interpretations.

Dutch or English? This is a basic question which is not always easy to answer as many English designs were copied direct from the Dutch. As a generalisation English tiles have a richer, thicker, smoother glaze which has a bluish appearance due to the increased lead oxide content; whereas Dutch examples have a soft sandy body and a dry, white glaze which tends to craze due to a higher level of tin, and the blue and manganese colours are applied more strongly. In most cases the quality of painting on Dutch tiles is good and sometimes with the help of elaborate pricked transfers, can be quite excellent, but somehow the English tiles achieve a spontaneous warmth and humour that is often lacking in their European counterparts.

The three main areas of production in England were London, Bristol and Liverpool. The decorators were known to move around, and sometimes the same designs were made at all three centres (p. 86 nos. **503, 504, 505**), therefore one cannot rely on subject matter alone for identifying the place of manufacture. To add to this problem it is known that a certain James Stowell sold Liverpool delftware in Bristol and advertised in Felix Farley's journal 2nd December 1752:

> "To be sold wholesale or retail . . .
> . . . all sorts of Liverpool tiles and
> wares . . ."

The Barred Ox-head corner motif (p. 27) which is copied directly from the Dutch, is the most common found on English tiles. It remained popular throughout the 18th century particularly in London but identification of factories for the earlier 18th century tiles is perhaps not quite so clear. In most instances these tiles have been attributed to a London manufacturer which can be supported to an extent from Garner's shards (Ray, p. 98-99) and Cockell's Vauxhall discoveries (E.C.C. Vol. 9, Part 2, 1974). However there are several varieties of this corner, for example (p. 95, nos. **559, 560, 561**) illustrates three quite different styles. Are these the produce of different London factories or were some of these tiles made in Liverpool? The first Liverpool delftware potters came from London and would be producing similar wares but unfortunately little is known. It seems likely that Bristol would have also made quantities of this popular design although only one (no. **97**) has been attributed in this catalogue. Consequently attributions given in this catalogue for the earlier 18th century tiles with Ox-head corners are tentative.

It does seem however that in many cases the corner motif remained a local feature and certain specific groups can be identified from this. Some of those more easily recognisable are listed on page 11.

A. London.** 1720-50.
12.9 x 0.7 cms. Blue.

B. Liverpool.** 1750-70.
12.7 x 0.7 cms. Blue.

No. **A** is a typical London tile with the common Barred Ox-head corner. The glaze is thick and shiny and there are signs of two diagonally opposite pinholes. This tile is probably some 30 years older than the Liverpool tile, no. **B**, which has the same scene. The octagonal dash border was often used at Liverpool and the blue has characteristically sunk into the surface of the glaze. Note the two swimming birds which is another Liverpool feature.

C. London.** 1760-90.
12.8 x 0.7 cms. Blue.

D. London.** 1760-90.
13.1 x 0.6 cms. Blue.

E. Bristol.** 1750-70.
13 x 0.8 cms. (approx). Blue.

F. Bristol.** 1750-70.
13 x 0.8 cms. (approx.) Blue.

The same figure appears on all these tiles although two are London and two are Bristol. Tile **C** is similar to nos. **147-148** and tile **D** has the same Diaper corners as nos. **93-96.** Both are strongly painted on a duck egg blue ground which is found on London tiles of the second half of the 18th century.
Tiles **E** and **F** have the usual Bristol Flowerhead corner but the figure has been superimposed on different backgrounds.

Typical **London corners:**	Barred Ox-head (p. 27)
	Dotted Flowerhead (p. 60)
	Carnation with Powdered border (p. 22)
	Diaper (p. 30)

During the first half of the 18th century the Barred Ox-head corner was by far the most common design and was still being used right through to the end of the century (see notes on p. 9). The corner was usually used with European landscape scenes or religious subjects. Liverpool produced a more refined version of this corner (p. 36) as did Bristol (no. **97**).

The London tiles that were made during the first half of the 18th century have a rough back and are sometimes a little warped, they have a thick white glaze often pinkish in colour which tends to pool along the edges with little pockmarks on the surface. Quite obvious on all these tiles are two diagonally opposite pinholes always on the front. Tiles with the Carnation corner and Powdered border (p. 22) have been excavated on the site of the Vauxhall pottery Lambeth. The Dotted Flowerhead corner (p. 60) has been found in Lambeth (Ray, fig. 27A p. 99).

By the middle of the century the glaze had become much more blue and towards the last quarter of the 18th century, more of a duck egg blue with heavy dark blue designs. By this date the tiles were more evenly made with smoother backs and no pinholes (p. 38).

Typical **Bristol corners:**	Flowerhead (p. 31 nos. **98-101**)
	Extended Flowerhead (p. 33)

The Flowerhead corner appears to have only been made at Bristol. Some of the earlier examples are quite small (nos. **98-99**) and have rough backs similar to the London tiles but there are rarely any sign of pinholes. The glaze has a rather matt and thin appearance, often with a grey bluish tone. Tiles with the typical Bristol painting in the "Bowen" style can be fairly accurately dated to between 1750 to 1770 (pp. 33-35). These are always well made with straight cut edges, being thick and larger than average and often with four or two pinholes quite clearly on the reverse. The very smooth texture of the backs make these tiles an easily recognisable group.

Typical **Liverpool corners:**	Barred Ox-head (p. 36 nos. **140-146**)
	Flowerhead with circle (p. 36 no. **138**)
	Barbed Medallion (p. 55 nos. **296-298**)
	Leaf (p. 53 nos. **275-277**)
	Trellis (p. 55 no. **294**)
	Michaelmas Daisy (p. 58 nos. **309-310**)
	Buttercup (p. 57 nos. **302-305**)
	Fish Roe (p. 58 nos. **311-314**)
	Dandelion (p. 25 nos. **55-60**)
	Ragged Flower (p. 25 nos. **61-63**)
	Cherub (p. 41 nos. **187-188**)
	Floral Ground (p. 41 nos. **185-186**)
	Louis XV and variations (p. 44-45)
	Octagonal Dash (p. 42)

Liverpool made by far the largest range of border designs, but these were mostly produced during the second half of the 18th century. (Those made earlier were probably very similar to London tiles and are therefore difficult to identify.) A refined Barred Ox-head corner was often used with flowers and European landscape scenes (nos. **140-146**). They were also used with the polychrome bird tiles (nos. **293** and **295**), as were the Barbed Medallion (nos. **296-298**), Leaf (nos. **275-277**) and Trellis designs (no. **294**). The Michaelmas Daisy (nos. **309-310**), Buttercup (nos. **302-305**) and Fish Roe (nos. **311-314**) borders are usually associated with chinoiserie figures. The Dandelion (nos. **55-60**) and Ragged Flower (nos. **61-63**) were normally used with a Powdered border and were popular with general landscape subjects, the latter also being used with religious scenes (no. **490**). The Cherub (nos. **187-188**), Floral Ground (nos. **185-186**) and Louis XV designs (pp. 44-45) were also usually confined to European landscape scenes. The Octagonal Dash border (p. 42) was used with a variety of subjects but may also have been used at Bristol.

Liverpool tiles are usually quite well made and in some cases the backs have a more porous appearance. Often numbers are painted on the reverse in blue, manganese, black and green. The decoration varies from very dark to pale, and sometimes the pigments have a tendency to sink into the surface of the glaze leaving indentations. A typical element in the Liverpool landscape scene is the stylized swans (cf. no. **137**). Sometimes very discreet diagonal pinholes are evident on the front of the tiles. Towards the end of the 18th century the tiles have a tendency to be thinner and are more mechanically made.

A star system has been used in order to facilitate the identification of tiles:
*** A certain attribution based on archaeological evidence or through comparison with other pieces whose identification is not disputed.
** The most probable place of manufacture based on comparison with other delftware.
* The most likely attribution although a degree of uncertainty remains.

No star means the place of manufacture is uncertain. Although an attribution has been given in the text this should be taken as a suggestion.

"PAVING TYLES"

During the mid 16th century it was fashionable for the Church and very wealthy throughout Europe to have highly decorated floors made up from ceramic or marble. With the introduction of tinglazed "paving tyles" it became possible for the middle classes to imitate this grandeur.

When the first Flemish potters arrived in Norwich in the 1560's, one of their products was "Paving Tyles" (page 5). A tile in the Victoria & Albert Museum (cf. Ray, no. 1), is thought to have been made in Norwich by Jansen and Andries for Sir Nicholas Bacon who built himself a mansion at Gorhambury, near St. Albans between 1563 and 1568. Another tile that may also have been made at Jansen's workshop was recovered in the 19th century from the site of Limpsfield New Hall, a house built by William Gresham between 1558 and 1579 (E.C.C. Vol. 11 Part 2, 1982). The tile (no. **1**) includes the initials WG and the Gresham grasshopper. (The same grasshopper appears on an early 17th century tile (no. **5**) which was recovered from the site of Baynards Castle, Upper Thames Street).

Jacob Jansen moved from Norwich to London and between 1571 and 1615, he was working at Aldgate. It is known that 13 other Flemish potters were working in and around that area and it is therefore assumed that paving tyles were also made here. The interesting collection of early tiles that have been gathered together by the Museum of London from various sources throughout the City of London (Britton, pp. 170-175) must be considered in this light, but what was made where is very difficult to say as the locally made tiles were very similar to those being made on the Continent. Tile no. 3 is typical in style to an Antwerp tile picture but also very similar to a tile found in the City of London. (Britton, no. 182). Tile no. 4 is well painted and may have been made in Antwerp, but this should be compared with a tile of the same pattern decorated by a less mature hand, that was found in Leadenhall Street, and has been attributed to Southwark. (Britton, no. 197).

In the 1950's during redevelopment work in Southwark a large quantity of delftware, which included kiln waste was discovered near the site of Christian Wilhelm's factory at Pickleherring Quay (the finds have been described in Ivor Noël Hume's excellent book, "Early English Delftware from London and Virginia"). Amongst the debris was a number of medallion tiles similar to nos **6,7,8** and **9**. Some of those recovered were obvious wasters (Hume, colour Pl. 20), and there can be no doubt that these were made locally although copying a Flemish design. The Museum of London has a number of these tiles which have been recovered from various sources, (Britton, pp. 172-173) and others have been excavated at Basing House, Hampshire ("Post Medieval Archaeology", Vol. 4, 1970, pp. 87-88).

The pattern of tile no. **11** is one of the most common found at Pickleherring Quay being produced in blue as well as polychrome (Hume, p. 56). This design has also been found on a tile recovered during excavations for the rebuilding of the Royal Exchange in 1848 (Britton, p. 196). These tiles are comparatively thin (1.2 cms.) and they have no sign of wear on the surface, which suggests that they were intended as wall tiles. A major source of clay for the London delftware potteries came by sea from Yarmouth (which also supplied Holland) (Britton, p. 12). The tiles no. **11** are labelled "from Great Yarmouth" and it seems reasonable to assume that they reached that destination as ballast on a return barge trip. The fashion for "paving tyles" had ceased by the middle of the 17th century.

PAVING TYLES

1. Possibly Norwich. Circa 1565
13.6 x 1.8 cms. Polychrome, Blue, Yellow and Green. (Reproduced by kind permission of Surrey Archaeological Society).

A fragment of a "paving tyle" recovered in the 19th century from the site of Limpsfield New Hall, a house built by William Gresham between 1558 and 1579. The decoration includes the initials WG and the Gresham grasshopper. Possibly from the workshop of Jansen and Andries. Compare with the "Nicolas Bacon" tile (Ray, no. 1). (E.C.C. Vol. II Part 2, 1982).

2. London or Flemish.
Second half 16th/early 17th century.
13.8 x 1.6 cms. Polychrome, Green, Blue, Ochre.

This fragment was recovered from the Thames foreshore in London. The body is a pale buff with a pitted back and with the edges chamfered. The pattern is very similar to a tile found on the site of Limpsfield New Hall (see notes relating to tile **1**).

3. Antwerp, possibly London.
Second half 16th century.
13.5 x 1.5 cms. Polychrome, Blue, Ochre, Yellow, Lime green.

This tile has a hard grey body and the surface is worn (cf. Britton, no. 182).

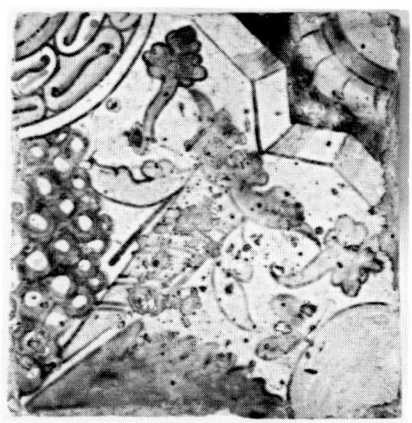

4. Possibly Antwerp.
Second half 16th/early 17th century.
13.4 x 1.6 cms. Polychrome, Blue, Yellow, Green.

Similar body to previous tile and also with a worn surface. The Museum of London have two similar tiles, one from Leadenhall Street (Britton, no. 197) and the other from Armoury House (86.66/19 (i)).

5. Probably London.
Early 17th century.
13.1 x 1.5 cms. Polychrome. (Reproduced by kind permission of the Museum of London, MOL no. 30.155).

The grasshopper is the device of the Gresham family. Compare with tile no. **1**. Similar medallion tiles from the Museum of London Collection are illustrated in (Britton, pp. 172-3). This tile was recovered from the site of Baynards Castle. Upper Thames St. in 1930.

The body of these tiles is a patchy pale brick colour and the front surfaces are worn, (cf. Britton, pp. 172-3). Excavations at Basing House (Post Medieval Archaeology, Vol. 4 1970, pp. 87-88) recovered some very similar tiles and another painted with a camel which is obviously a waster was recovered from the Pickleherring Quay site in Southwark (Hume, p. 19).

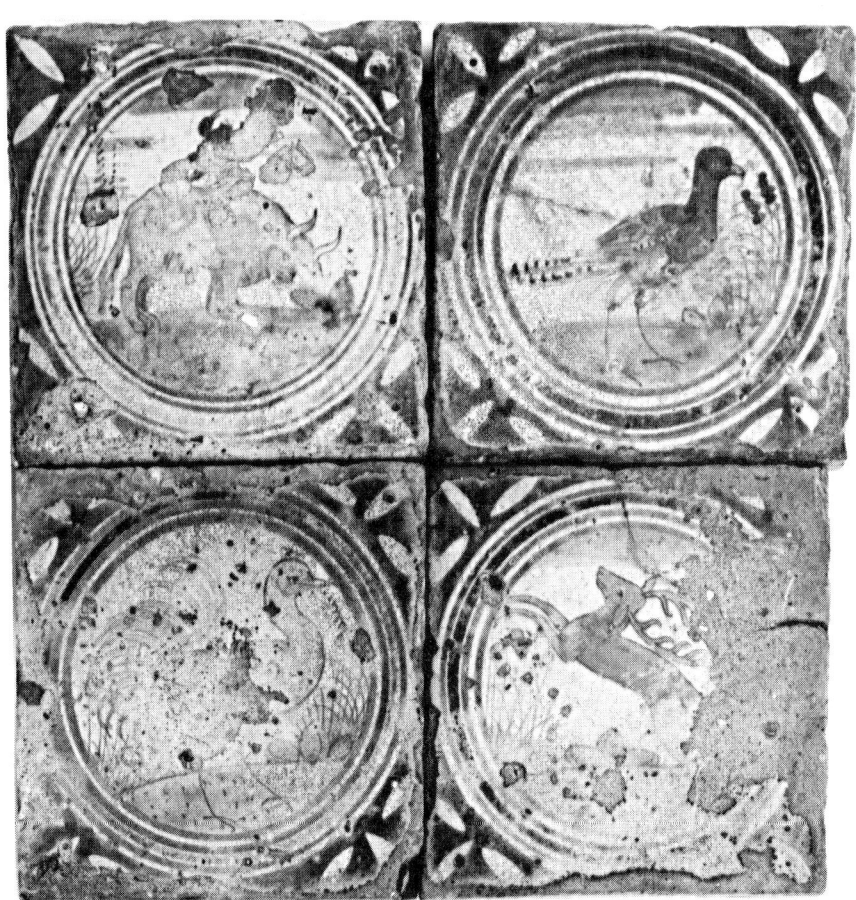

6, 7, 8, 9. Probably London.
Early 17th century.
Approx 13.6 x 1.9 cms. Polychrome,
Blue, Manganese, Ochre, Green, Yellow.

London/Flemish

10. London or Flemish.
Early 17th century.
4.6 x 6.5 x 1.6 cms. Blue.

This unusual corner tile was recovered from the Thames at Three Cranes Wharf. The edges are straight cut and it is very similar to a slightly larger corner tile in the London Museum (Britton, no. 198).

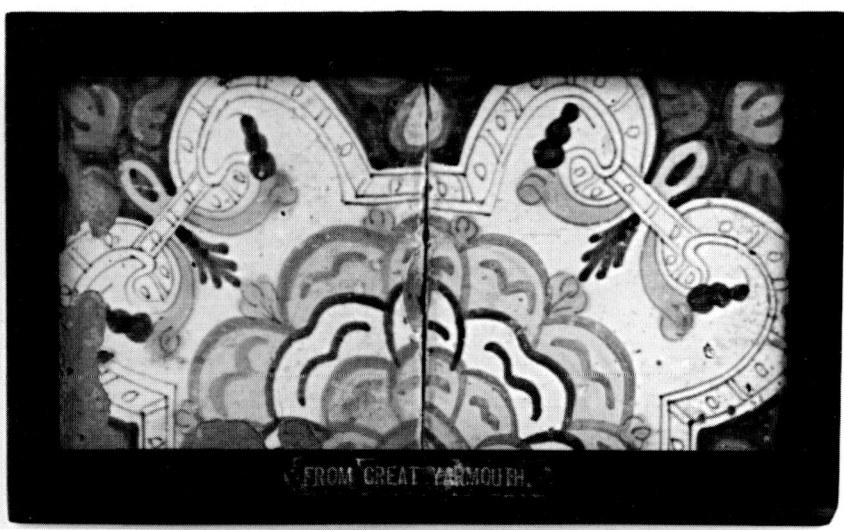

11. Probably London.
First half 17th century.
13.3 x 1.2 cms. approx. Polychrome,
Blue, Lime Green, Ochre, Yellow.

These tiles are labelled "From Great Yarmouth" (see notes on p. 13). The comparative thinness and lack of wear suggests that they were used for the wall. Although a Flemish pattern, this was one of the most common designs found at Pickleherring Quay, Southwark (Hume, p. 19, 56) (cf. Britton, no. 196.)

WALL TILES

In 1676 Jan Ariens Van Hamme, a potter from Delft, obtained a patent "to exercise his Art of Makeinge Tiles and Porcelane and other earthenwares after the way practised in Holland". He died in about 1680 and it has been suggested that he started a delftware factory at Copthall, Lambeth (Britton, p. 159). This assumption is based on a letter dated 1677 (Ray, p. 35) which confirms that "Holland tiles" were being made in Vauxhall and this may be a reference to Van Hamme's factory. The letter further states that the London potteries were having difficulty in their production of tiles.

At about this time a series of playing cards were produced which graphically illustrate scenes from the "Popish Plot"; a notorious conspiracy in 1678 to kill King Charles II and establish a Catholic minority*. Several sets of tiles were made with scenes that were directly copied from these contemporary playing cards and were finely painted in the "Holland" style (no. **12**). It has therefore been assumed that Van Hamme's factory produced these tiles being the only one capable of this quality at that time.

(For further information on the Popish Plot see Ray, p. 61).

*NOTE: There was always a serious threat of a Catholic revival and the illustrating of the conspiracy on playing cards was useful anti-Catholic propaganda. A similar set of cards are known showing the "Gunpowder Plot" which were made for the same purpose.

12. London.* Possibly Copthall. Circa 1680.
12.7 x 0.8 cms. Bright Blue. Inscribed "The Plot first hatcht at Rome by the Pope and Cardinalls &$^{c\text{t}}$". One from a set illustrating scenes from the Popish Plot, copied from contemporary playing cards.

This subject is taken from the Ace of Hearts (cf. Ray, 8). For further discussion on these tiles see (Ray, p. 114) and (Britton, p. 176). Part of a set of "Popish Plot" tiles was sold at Sotheby's 15 March 1971, but these are without a border and less finely painted (cf. Ray, 18).

Surprisingly few English tiles have been attributed to the period 1680-1700. It is known that there were problems with production but this also proves that tiles were being made. These early tiles would be similar to the Dutch and not easy to identify, and it is not until the early 18th century that the English tiles become more distinct.

13. Possibly English/London. Late 17th century.
13 x 0.9 cms. Blue.

This fisherman appears on delftware tiles throughout the 18th century but the pinky glaze suggests this is early. The corner motif is unusual for English tiles but when compared with similar Dutch tiles this example has a denser, heavier feel. A similar tile with a scene closely resembling tile no. **80** was found at New Castle, the old colonial capital of Delaware, on the site of the English Courthouse which was built around 1689.

London

14. London.* Late 17th century.
12.7 x 0.9 cms. Bright Blue. Christ appearing to Mary Magdalene. Ray (no. 95), says that this is not a Dutch design. It is also unusual to find Christ depicted without a halo.

An early date has been attributed to tile **14** because of its thick pinky white glaze which is a characteristic of late 17th century London delftware and is similar to the glaze used on drug jars of this period. Another early feature is the **"Spider head corner"**, a motif rarely used on the later English tiles (for an early 18th century Spider head corner see no. **69**). The potter has had trouble with the glaze and the same problem has been experienced with a similar manganese fragment found by Garner at Lambeth (cf. Ray, fig. 25C). The Glaisher Collection has a round flat stand which is dated '1686' and is decorated with "religious" figures painted in a similar way (Lipski, no. 1553).
For other 17th century tiles, see nos. **435, 474, 532, 533, 536, 625** and **629**.

15. London.* Late 17th century.
12.5 x 0.9 cms. Blue. Christ at the Column. Again Christ has no halo. The glaze is rather thick and slaty in colour, the figures are outlined in a very dark manganese often found on delft of this period. The surface is rather lumpy and poorly fired. There are two pinholes on the front and the edges are cut straight. (cf. no. **629**).

16. London.** 1700-20.
13 x 0.9 cms. Blue. A similar decorated tile with sponged trees and with the same unusual corners is in the Ashmolean Museum (cf. Ray, Pl.12 p. 135). The style of painting is typical of that found on delftware in London during the early part of the 18th century. Compare with figures on a mug dated 1707 (Lipski, no. 947).

18TH CENTURY TILES

EUROPEAN FIGURES AND LANDSCAPE SCENES

Powdered Ground Tiles

The powdered manganese decoration was popular on delftware during the first half of the 17th century. This style then went out of fashion in England and does not reappear until the second quarter of the 18th century the earliest dated pieces being 1739. Some of the tiles illustrated here may be a little earlier than this date in an attempt to copy the Dutch powdered manganese tiles that were being produced during the late 17th and early 18th century. The powdered blue ground was never made in Holland.

Before the powder was applied cut out shapes were placed on the tiles which resulted in certain areas being left blank. The shapes were then removed and the undecorated areas painted over. On the later tiles the powdering tends to be finer.

17. London.** 1725-50.
12.9 x 0.8 cms. Blue, powdered Mauve.

18. London.** 1725-50.
12.8 x 0.8 cms. Blue, powdered Manganese. (cf. no. **76**).

19. London.** 1725-50.
13 x 0.9 cms. Polychrome figure of Ceres in red, green & blue, red corners. Bright powdered blue. High gloss. Compare with the plate illustrated in Fig. II and with the tiles illustrated on page 61.

No. **17** is painted very much in the Dutch style and has an unusual coloured border. Ray (no. 115), illustrates a tile of similar colouring which he suggests is Bristol, but the Cherub corners are so close to those on the flower tile no. **337** that it is probably London. No. **18** is painted in the more typical manganese tone. No. **19** has the **Carnation corner** which has been at Vauxhall (E.C.C. Vol 9 Part 2; E.C.C. Vol 11 Part 1).

Fig. II A London** delftware plate, diameter 21cm., painted in a dark blue, showing 'Ceres' surrounded by a border of cherub heads. The style of painting is closely related to a plate dated 1737 (Lipski, no. 419).

Bristol/Liverpool/Glasgow

20. Bristol.*** 1725-50.
13 x 0.9 cms. Blue, dark Mauve/Manganese powdering. The mauve-manganese is distinctive and a fragment of a very similar tile was found at the Lime Kiln Lane potteries, Brandon Hill, Bristol (Ray fig. 29 p. 101). Ray also illustrates two others of this type (cf. Ray no. 113 and 114). The subject of a man carrying a basket was also used on London tiles.

21. Liverpool.* 1725-50.
12.5 x 1.0 cms. Blue Glossy. This is a substantial tile and is not unlike the London tiles on page 61. A fragment with the "Dandelion corner" has been found in Liverpool (Ray fig. 31). Compare with the later tiles on page 25.

22. Liverpool. 1725-50.
12.6 x 1.0 cms. Dark Blue, Pale Manganese powder. The quarter round "Rosette corner" was popular on Dutch tiles of the late 17th-early 18th century. This tile compares with the early London and Bristol tiles in this section but the colouring is slightly unusual and Ray (no. 118) illustrates a similar tile but with the "Dandelion corner" which is a characteristic of Liverpool (Ray fig. 31E p. 103). The design is similar to that on the London tile **18,** but with only one figure.

23. Bristol.* 1725-50.
13 x 0.9 cms. Blue, powdered pale Mauve. This has an unusual pale powdered border and the central scene is delicately painted in the Dutch style. Ray (no. 233) illustrates a similar border of twelve scallops with quarter rosette corners, fragments of which have been found at Lime Kiln Lane, Bristol (Ray fig. 29c p. 101).

24. Glasgow.* Circa 1750.
12.8 cms. sq. approx. Blue with powdered Manganese. Recovered from the grounds of Glenarbuck House, Glasgow. See notes on page 8 and compare with Fig. I. Reproduced by kind permission of The Peoples Palace, Glasgow.

London/Bristol/Liverpool

25, 26, 27, 28. Possibly Bristol. 1725-50.
12.7 x 1.0 cms. Blue. Powdered Manganese. These scenes are typical of those found on Frisian tiles of the late 17th-early 18th century, but the examples illustrated have English characteristics. **25** and **26** have a pinky background and have had trouble with the glaze running. Tiles **27** and **28** have a bluey background and are better made without any pinholes.

29. Bristol.** 1725-50.
12.4 x 0.8 cms. Blue. Powdered Mauve. (cf. Ray no. 225). Finely pitted, thin glaze.

30. Bristol.** 1725-50.
12.4 x 0.8 cms. Blue. Powdered Manganese. (Compare with Ray, nos. 110-111). The glaze is similar to no. **29**.

31. London.** 1725-50.
12.5 x 0.9 cms. approx. Darkish Blue. Powdered Manganese. Very similar to nos. **33-36.** cf. no. **80.**

32. Liverpool.* 1740-60.
12.7 x 0.8 cms. Blue. Dark Powdered. Manganese. These quarter rosette corners are slightly more complex than other examples on this page. For another similar tile but with the "dandelion corner" (cf. Ray no. 118) also (Horne no. 29). cf. no. **233.**

These tiles have the **"Quarter Rosette corner"**. The powdered mauve on Bristol tile, no. **29** seems to be an early feature as does the small size (cf. Ray, no. 225). No. **30** is also probably Bristol and compares with Ray (no. 111). No. **31** is painted with a typical London scene, compare the painting with nos. **33-36**. Similar tile fragments have been found at Lambeth (Ray, p. 99, fig. 26). The glaze on **29** and **30** is thin and finely pitted whereas **31** is much more thick and shiny.

London

33, 34 London.** 1740-60.
35, 36 12.7 x 0.9 cms. approx. Darkish Blue, Powdered Manganese. Four tiles with **"Carnation corners"** decorated with typical landscape scenes often found on London delftware during the 18th century. See notes on carnation corners on page 24.

37, 38, 39 London.** 1740-60.
40, 41, 42 12.5 x 0.7 cms. approx. Darkish Blue. Powdered Manganese. The quality of painting is exceptional when compared with the more conventional nos. **33-36**.

This selection of London tiles have an affinity with the flower tiles on pages 61 and 62 and illustrates some of the variations and colours that were available. For a note on the carnation corner see page 24.

43. London.** 1740-60.
12.9 x 0.9 cms. Blue, Powdered Manganese.

44. London.** 1740-60.
12.9 x 0.9 cms. All Blue.

45. London.** 1740-60.
12.9 x 0.8 cms. All Manganese.

These three are all the same size and thickness and are painted in rather strong colours.

46. London.* 1740-60.
12.5 x 0.9 cms. Blue, Powdered Manganese.

47. London.** 1740-60.
13.0 x 0.8 cms. Blue, Powdered Red.

48. London.** 1740-60.
12.7 x 0.8 cms. Manganese, Powdered Blue.

No. **46** can be compared with tiles **33-36**, but has unusual Petal corners. No. **47** has a powdered red border which is rare (cf. **337**) whereas no. **48** is painted in manganese with a bright powdered blue.

49. London.** 1740-60.
12.5 x 0.8 cms. Blue, Powdered Manganese.

50. London.** 1740-60.
12.7 x 0.8 cms. All Blue.

51. London.** 1740-60.
12.6 x 0.8 cms. Blue, Powdered Manganese.

The Quarter Rosette corner on no. **50** is more common on earlier tiles. No. **51** is painted with a typical harbour scene and has one of the carnations unfinished.

London

Fig. III. A delftware plate decorated in blue with powdered Manganese. Diameter 22.5 cms. Circa 1740. London.** (Reproduced by kind permission of Bristol Museum & Art Gallery). For a similar plate dated 1741 see (Lipski no. 475).

The carnation decoration is similar to that found on the tiles illustrated on pages 22-24. Traditionally powdered manganese plates of this type have been attributed to Bristol! (Bristol Collection—nos. 15, 26, 27, 30, 31, 32, 46 and 49). However it seems likely that some of these were made in London as tiles with the Carnation corner have been recovered from Fore Street in Lambeth (Ray, p. 99 fig. 27B) and from Vauxhall (Britton, p. 71 fig. 12K). The central motif on this plate was also used on tile no. **425** and a similar pattern appears on the recess tile no. **668**. However tile no. **300**, on page 56, and no. **343** on page 63 should be considered as possibly Bristol.

52. London.** 1760-80.
12.7 x 0.75 cms. Blue. Powdered Manganese.

53. London.** 1760-80.
12.7 x 0.75 cms. Blue. Powdered Manganese.

54. London.** 1760-80.
12.7 x 0.75 cms. Blue. Powdered Manganese.

Compared with nos. **43-51,** these tiles are well cut and flatter and have no pinholes. The glaze is more even with a duck egg blue tone to the background and the application of the powdered blue is very much finer.
The scene of a watermill, no. **52**, appears on an earlier London tile (cf. Ray, no. 247) and the man skating and smoking no. **53** has been copied from a Dutch design. The man fishing with a net no. **54** also appears on a tile with the octagonal dash border (Ray, 190) which may be a Liverpool tile copying a London design or a London tile using the octagonal dash border!

Liverpool

55. Liverpool.** 1740-60.
12.7 x 0.6 cms. Bright Blue.

56. Liverpool.** 1740-60.
12.7 x 0.7 cms. Blue. Powdered Manganese.

57. Liverpool.** 1740-60.
12.5 x 0.7 cms. Blue. Powdered Manganese.

58. Liverpool.** 1740-60.
12.5 x 0.7 cms. Blue. Powdered Blue.

59. Liverpool.** 1750-75.
12.7 x 0.6 cms. Blue. Powdered Blue.

60. Liverpool.** 1750-75.
12.6 x 0.6 cms. Blue. Powdered Manganese.

The **"Dandelion corner"** has been found at Liverpool (Ray, fig. 31E p. 103) and is often used with typical Liverpool scenes. The scalloped border **56** is fairly uncommon (pp. 20-21) and the squashed Carnation corner on **59** is rare (cf. Ray, no. 240). The seated shepherd on **60** is a common character on Liverpool tiles. A label on the back of this tile reads "obtained from an old timber-framed inn with coachyard in Brittox, Devizes".

61. Liverpool.** 1750-75.
12.6 x 0.6 cms. Blue.

62. Liverpool.** 1750-75.
12.8 x 0.8 cms. Blue.

63. Liverpool.** 1750-75.
12.9 x 0.8 cms. Blue.

A fragment of a tile with the **"Ragged Flower corner"** with powdered blue edges has been found at Liverpool, (cf. Ray p. 103, fig. 31). The scene of a Gentleman and Lady with a fan no. **61**, has been copied from an earlier London tile (cf. Ray, 124). Compare with the tiles, nos. **64-65**.

London

64. London.** 1710-30.
12.7 x 0.9 cms. Dark Blue.

The style of painting on **64** is the same as that on a plate dated 1714 (Fig. IV p. 28). The painting is on a pinky white background, thick and glossy and similar in appearance to the large tile pictures on page 114-115. Note the dark trekking of the trees and foliage which is an early feature and quite unlike the painting on tile no. **68**, which has a much more milky white background and is later. For a later Liverpool version of this subject (cf. Horne, no. 12) which is the same series as no. **63**.

65. London.** 1710-40.
Dark Blue. Other tiles are also known with this unusual "**Angel Head corner**", including **64**. The stone palisade is a feature that appears in most of these 'Dutch' scenes. (cf. no. **485**).

66. London.** 1720-40.
12.8 x 0.8 cms. Blue, rather worn.

67. London.** 1730-50.
12.8 x 0.9 cms. Bright Blue.

Other tiles from this group are illustrated in (Horne, nos. 2 and 3; Britton, no. 207; Ray, nos. 122, 123 and 124). A fragment from a similar tile was found at Vauxhall by Denis Cockell (E.C.C. Vol 9 Part 2, Pl. 136). These same subjects were copied at Liverpool, compare with no. **61** also (cf. Horne, nos. 10, 11 & 12 and Ray, no. 189).

68. London.** 1740-60.
12.8 x 0.8 cms. Bright Blue.

For other all over landscape scenes see page 37.

69. London. 1720-50.
Misty Blue. This unusual tile has the Spider Head corner which was not often used on English tiles (cf. 14-15).

The **"Barred Ox-head corner"** is copied from the Dutch and was by far the most common design being used throughout the 18th century. This corner motif was used at Bristol and Liverpool and therefore there is a degree of uncertainty on some of the attributions (see notes on page 9).

70. London.* 1720-50.
12.5 x 0.8 cms. Strong Blue on pinky ground.

71. London.* 1720-50.
12.5 x 0.8 cms. Strong Blue on pinky ground.

These are attributed to London because of their rough back and pinky glaze, although similar subjects appear on Bristol tiles and the design continued to be used throughout the 18th century.

72. London.** 1720-50.
12.9 x 0.8 cms. Blue.

73. London.** 1720-50.
12.9 x 0.8 cms. Strong Blue.

The subject of a man shooting ducks has been found at Vauxhall (E.C.C. Vol 9 Part 2, P1.135). No. **73** has slightly different corners and the glaze is rather grey and thin. The same scene of a man fishing but in reverse, has also been found on a tile fragment from Vauxhall.

74. London.** 1720-50.
12.0 x 1.0 cms. Shiny Blue.

75. London.* 1730-50.
16.2 x 1.6 cms. Greyish Blue.

These two tiles illustrate the extremes in size that were made. No. **74** is one of a group of small thick tiles, see no. **622** also (cf. Horne, nos. 4-8 and 46). No. **75** is an exceptionally large tile. The only other example of this size known is decorated in a similar way with a figure of a man leaning on a stick within a landscape (illustrated in E.C.C. Vol 11 Part 2, P1. 74d). The size of this tile draws one's attention to the very hard body. Batty Langley, the architect, wrote in 1748 complaining of the hardness of London tiles: "But I think not any of them can be rubb'd and gaged with neatness as can be with Dutch Tiles, unless they have very lately made that improvement by moderately opening the Body of their clay with Woolwich sand" (Ray, p. 38).

London

76. London.** 1720-50.
13 x 0.8 cms. Blue. cf. no. **18**.

Fig. IV. A delftware plate initialed and dated '$^B_{TA}$ 1714' Diameter 21.6 cms. London**
(Reproduced by kind permission of the Birmingham City Museum and Art Gallery).
It is unusual to find the same scene on a plate and a tile. This subject was used throughout the 18th century on London tiles, see no. **83**. The style of painting, which is typical of this period, can be compared with tile no. **64** and **164** and also at Liverpool cf. no. **170**.

77. London. 1720-50.
13.0 x 0.9 cms. Blue.

78. London.** 1720-50.
12.8 x 0.9 cms. Strong Blue.

79. London.** 1730-60.
13 x 0.8 cms. Manganese.

No. **77** may possibly be London although the "horns" of the Ox-head corners are turned sharply inwards, which is typical of the later Liverpool tiles.

Ships on London tiles are rare. The corners on no. **79** are unusual but the rich glaze suggests this is also London.

Fig. V. A tinglazed "flower brick" decorated in blue with a similar scene to tile no. **81**. Length 14 cms. x 5.5 cms. Height 8 cms., circa 1750 London.**

80. London.** 1740-60.
12.4 x 0.7 cms. Blue.
cf. no. **31** and notes on no. **13**.

81. London.** 1740-60.
12.9 x 0.7 cms. Manganese.
cf. Fig. V.

82. London.** 1740-60.
12.4 x 0.6 cms. Blue.

83. London.** 1740-60.
13 x 0.7 cms. Manganese.
Compare with Fig. IV.

84. London.** 1740-60.
13 x 0.7 cms. Manganese.

85. London.** 1740-60.
13 x 0.6 cms. Manganese.

86. London.** 1740-60.
12.8 x 0.7 cms. Blue.

87. London.** 1740-60.
12.6 x 0.7 cms. Blue.

88. London.** 1740-60.
12.9 x 0.8 cms. Blue.

These tiles represent a large group of European landscape subjects that were made in London and were popular during the 18th century, the same scenes reappearing time and again. A very similar horse and cart no. **81** appears on the Butcher's Bowl at the Ashmolean Museum which is dated 1753 (Lipski, no. 1138) also cf. Fig. V. The shepherd playing a pipe, no. **83,** and the miller carrying his sack, no. **84,** appear amongst the later tiles on page 38 and were also used at Liverpool, nos. **168-170**. The back view of a man pointing, no. **85,** was also used on Bristol and Liverpool tiles, see nos. **108** and **104** respectively. Tiles **86, 87, 88** are all executed by the same person, note the distinctive way the trees have been painted.

London

89. London.** 1760-90.
12.5 x 0.7 cms. Blue.

90. London.** 1760-90.
12.6 x 0.8 cms. Blue.

91. London.** 1760-90.
12.5 x 0.7 cms. Blue.

92. London.** 1760-90.
12.5 x 0.9 cms. Blue.

These later tiles are painted in an inky blue on a bluish background. They are well cut and are more mechanically made having no sign of pinholes. The figure in no. **90** is carrying an eel trap which must have been a common sight on the Thames during the 18th century cf. no. **157**. The Barred Ox-head corner forms an attractive decoration when put together with others of its kind.

93. London. 1760-90.
13 x 0.7 cms. Blue.

94. London. 1760-90.
13 x 0.7 cms. Blue.

95. London. 1760-90.
13 x 0.7 cms. Blue.

96. London. 1760-90.
13 x 0.7 cms. Blue.

The **"Diaper corner"** with a roundel appears only on late London tiles which are usually well made (cf. Ray, nos. 137, 138, 251 and Horne, no. 23). The man carrying a basket on no. **94** was often used, and appears on a fragment picked up by Garner in Lambeth (Ray fig. 24). The man carrying a sack, no. **95** is very similar to the miller, no. **84,** and the man on no. **96** is the same as on no. **160**. For a Liverpool Diaper corner see page 45.

97. Bristol.** Early 18th century.
12.5 x 0.7 cms. Blue.

The grey blue colour of the glaze and the thin finely pitted dry surface suggests Bristol. The trekking and painting style is characteristic of the late 17th and early 18th century delftware. The crudely painted Barred Ox-head corners are unusual but the quality of painting is similar to the powdered ground tile no. **30** and **343**. The same figure appears on no. **100**.

98. Bristol.** 1720-50.
12.4 x 0.8 cms. Mauve.

99. Bristol.** 1720-50.
12.4 x 0.8 cms. Mauve.

The **"Flowerhead corner"** was predominantly a Bristol design but may also have been used in London. A similar unusual mauve colour was also used on some of the powdered tiles cf. **20** and **29**. This may perhaps be a characteristic of Bristol.

100. Bristol.** 1720-50.
13 x 0.8 cms. Blue.

101. Bristol.** 1720-50.
13.2 x 0.8 cms. Blue.

The rather smudgy style of painting and dark blue Flowerhead corners are the same as on no. **107**. A similar scene to **100** has been used on the early tile no. **97**. Ray (no. **125** and **126**) illustrates two tiles with the same background as **100**, but with different figures transposed.

Bristol

102. Bristol.* 1740-70.
12.6 x 0.8 cms. Blue.

103. Bristol.** 1725-50.
13.2 x 0.9 cms. Manganese.

104. Bristol.* 1740-70.
12.5 x 0.7 cms. Manganese.

105. Bristol.** 1740-70.
13 x 0.7 cms. Manganese.

106. Bristol.** 1740-70.
13 x 0.8 cms. Manganese.

107. Bristol.** 1720-50.
13 x 0.8 cms. Blue.

108. Bristol.** 1740-70.
12.6 x 0.8 cms. (cut down). Blue.

109. Bristol.** 1740-70.
12.6 x 0.8 cms. (cut down). Blue.
Grenadier—a rare subject.

110. Bristol.** 1740-70.
12.6 x 8 cms. (cut down). Blue.

102 is slightly smaller than normal and the painting is not unlike the London tiles (nos. **151-152**), although this corner is usually associated with Bristol. The same scene appears on a tile with 'Barred Ox-head corners' illustrated in (Horne 27). **103** is an unusual subject of a house with a dovecote and it has slightly different corners. No. **107** has a flag which is similar to one on a powdered manganese plate dated 1740, (Lipski, nos. 565, 566, 567). The back view of a man pointing no. **108,** also appears on a London tile, no. **85,** and a Liverpool tile no. **144.** No. **109** and **110** are from the same set as nos. **E** and **F** on page 10. The Grenadier **109** is a very rare subject.

Bristol

111. Bristol.** 1750-70.
13 x 0.7 cms. Blue.

112. Bristol.** 1750-70.
13 x 0.8 cms. Manganese.

113. Bristol.** 1750-70.
13.2 x 0.7 cms. Blue.

114. Bristol.** 1750-70.
13.3 x 0.7 cms. Manganese.

115. Bristol.** 1750-70.
13 x 0.7 cms. Blue.

116. Bristol.** 1750-70.
13 x 0.8 cms. Manganese.

117. Bristol.** 1750-70.
13 x 0.8 cms. Blue.

118. Bristol.** 1750-70.
13.4 x 0.8 cms. Blue.

119. Bristol.** 1750-70.
13.5 x 0.8 cms. Blue.

These delicate scenes appear to be painted freehand without the use of a stencil (see notes on page 4). **112** and **116** are related as are **111** and **115**. No. **118** can be compared with the Bristol landscape tiles, nos. **153-4,** page 37. The boating scene on **119** is a common subject used on Bristol plates ("English Delftware in the Bristol Collection"—Britton, p. 278 and p. 282).

Bristol

Bristol/Liverpool

135. Bristol. *** 1750-70.
13.2 x 0.8 cms. Blue.

Fig. VI. A tinglazed plate decorated in blue with a European landscape scene. 20.5 cms. diameter. 1750-70. Bristol. ***
This popular scene appears on dated wares which range from 1753 to 1766 (Lipski, nos. 569-572, 619, 628, 1196, 1200).

136. Bristol. *** 1750-70.
13.3 x 0.8 cms. Blue.

137. Liverpool. ** 1750-75.
12.9 x 0.7 cms. Blue.

No. **136** is the same as the tiles on page 34, being very well made and with two pinholes on the back. No. **137** has a similar corner motif but in other respects is typically Liverpool. It is well made but slightly smaller with chamfered edges. The blue has sunk into the surface and the decoration includes the characteristic Liverpool swans.

Panel of 15 tiles.
120, 121, 122 Bristol. *** 1750-70.
123, 124, 125 13.3 x 0.8 cms. approx.
126, 127, 128 Blue.
129, 130, 131
132, 133, 134

These typical Bristol tiles are very well made with sharply cut corners and smooth backs. About half of these have four pinholes, always on the back with one in each corner, which is a significant Bristol feature; nos. **133** and **134** have had a dark magnanese added to the blue which is unusual. The distinctive quality and size is also found on some of the polychrome tiles, pages 51, 54, 59.

Liverpool

138. Liverpool.** 1750-75.
12.7 x 0.7 cms. Blue.

139. Liverpool.** 1750-75.
12.7 x 0.7 cms. Blue.

140. Liverpool.** 1750-75.
12.5 x 0.6 cms. Manganese.

141. Liverpool.** 1750-75.
12.7 x 0.6 cms. Blue.

142. Liverpool.** 1750-75.
12.6 x 0.6 cms. Manganese.

143. Liverpool.** 1750-75.
12.8 x 0.7 cms. Blue.

144. Liverpool.** 1750-75.
12.5 x 0.7 cms. Manganese.

145. Liverpool.** 1750-75.
12.6 x 0.7 cms. Blue.

146. Liverpool. 1750-75.
12.7 x 0.7 cms. Blue.

These are typical of many thousands of similar tiles produced at Liverpool using a variety of figures, houses, estuaries, boats, castles, etc., as subject matter, and all have versions of the "**Barred Ox-head**". Tiles **138** and **139** are by the same hand but have different corners. Tile **140** has rather spidery corners but this figure was often used on Liverpool tiles. The corners on **141** and **143** compare with the bird tiles nos. **293** and **295**. The pointing figure on no. **144** is very similar to the London tile no. **85** and the Bristol tile no. **108**. The stylized boats on a horizon achieved with three or four strokes of the brush is another Liverpool characteristic, see nos. **144**, **145** and **146**. No. **146** has been painted in two different shades, mainly blue and picked out in a dark bluey manganese almost like "trekking" to bring out the landscape and bushes. No. **140** has a number 9 in black on the back, and no. **145** is similarly marked with a large letter 'T'.

London/Bristol

Scenes painted without borders were common to London, Bristol and Liverpool. No. **147** and **148** are both painted with typical London scenes although the colour of the glaze on each tile is quite different, no. **147** being much pinker with a bright blue. The sailing barge, no. **149** is known with a powdered manganese border (cf. Ray, no. 319). No. **150** is probably quite late, having no pinholes and is similar to the tiles on page 38, although a tower with flag appears on an earlier Bristol tile, no. **107**.

147. London.** 1740-60.
12.4 x 0.8 cms. Bright Blue.

148. London.** 1740-60.
12.8 x 0.8 cms. Blue.

149. London.** 1740-70.
12.7 x 0.7 cms. Blue.

150. London.** 1760-80.
12.5 x 0.7 cms. Blue.

The lady by a tree, no. **151**, is painted very finely and could be mistaken for Bristol, but the scene is the same as tile no. **148**. The boatman in **152** which is from the same set, is known with powdered blue/carnation corners (cf. Horne, no. 52 and also Ray, no. 320). The glaze on these tiles is typically London with two pinholes on the front. For further London tiles painted without a border see pages 26 and 38.

No. **153** and **154** are Bristol and can be compared with the tiles on page 33. The man with a bundle no. **153**, is known with a variety of borders (cf. Ray, p. 141).

151. London.** 1740-70.
12.8 x 0.8 cms. Manganese.

152. London. 1740-70.
12.8 x 0.8 cms. Manganese.

153. Bristol.** 1740-70.
12.7 x 0.7 cms. Strong Blue.

154. Bristol.** 1740-70.
12.7 x 0.7 cms. Strong Blue.

London

155, 156, 157 Panel of 12 tiles.
158, 159, 160 London.** 1780-
161, 162, 163 1800.
164, 165, 166 13 x 0.7 cms. Blue.

These are well made tiles without any trace of pinholes and are painted in a rather intense blue. The painting can be compared with a mug dated 1793 (Lipski, no. 866). The patterns are typical of London and were used throughout the 18th century, no. **157**, the eel catcher, compares with no. **90**, and no. **159** is the same pattern as no. **85**. The scene on no. **164** is the same as the Liverpool tile no. **170**. The man carrying a sack, no. **166**, is a familiar character who also appears on no. **84** and the Liverpool tile no. **168**.

Liverpool

167. Liverpool.** 1750-75.
12.7 x 0.7 cms. Blue.

168. Liverpool.** 1750-75.
12.7 x 0.6 cms. Pale Blue.

169. Liverpool.** 1750-75.
12.5 x 0.6 cms. Pale Blue.

170. Liverpool.** 1750-75.
12.8 x 0.7 cms. Blue.
cf. Fig. IV, page 28.

171. Liverpool.** 1750-75.
12.7 x 0.7 cms. Blue.

172. Liverpool.** 1750-75.
12.6 x 0.7 cms. Manganese.

173. Liverpool.** 1750-75.
12.7 x 0.8 cms. Pale Blue.

174. Liverpool.* 1750-75.
12.6 x 0.8 cms. Blue.

175. Liverpool.** 1750-75.
13 x 0.6 cms. Blue

Apart from no. **174** all these tiles are the typical Liverpool products of the second half of the 18th century and none have pinholes. The miller with a sack, no. **168**, and shepherd, no. **170** are the same as London designs (cf. nos. **84** and **164**). The reclining lady, no. **173**, was often used on tiles (cf. Ray, no. 180 and 185) and appears on the outside of a bowl dated 1757 (Lipski 1167).
No. **174** is different from the others having two pinholes on the front and is painted in the Dutch style. In every other way it appears to be English, but does not fit into the London or Bristol categories.

Liverpool/Bristol

176. Liverpool.** 1750-75.
12.6 x 0.7 cms. Blue.

177. Liverpool.** 1750-55.
12.6 x 0.7 cms. Blue.

178. Liverpool.** 1750-55.
12.6 x 0.7 cms. Blue.

179. Liverpool.** 1750-75.
12.6 x 0.7 cms. Blue.

180. Liverpool.** 1750-75.
12.6 x 0.7 cms. Blue.

181. Liverpool.** 1750-75.
12.6 x 0.7 cms. Blue.

These six tiles illustrate the variety of eccentric and bizarre designs that were made at Liverpool in large quantities in both manganese and blue.

182. Bristol.** 1760-80.
13.5 x 0.6 cms. Blue.

The unusually large size suggests this is a Bristol tile and compares with those on page 34. Another tile from the same set had four pinholes, and the elongated tree is similar to that on tile no. **224.**

Bristol/Liverpool

183. Bristol. 1750-70.
13 x 0.9 cms. Manganese.

184. Liverpool. 1750-70.
12.5 x 0.8 cms. Dark Blue.

The **"Studded Border"** was painted at Bristol and Liverpool. The Bristol tile, no. **183,** has a more blue, slightly pitted glaze and can be compared with no. **223** and also (Ray, nos. 261 and 262). The Liverpool tile no. **184** has a whiter background and is the same as the flower tiles on page 64 (cf. Ray, no. 266). Compare with the recess tile no. **673.**

185. Liverpool. 1750-75.
12.7 x 0.8 cms. Dark Blue.

186. Liverpool. 1750-75.
12.6 x 0.7 cms. Dark Blue.

187. Liverpool.** 1750-75.
12.8 x 0.8 cms. Dark Blue.

188. Liverpool.** 1750-75.
12.8 x 0.8 cms. Dark Blue.

Tile no. **185** and **186** have very elaborate **"Floral Ground Border"** which must have taken ages to paint even with the help of a stencil (cf. Ray, Pl. 21). This design appears to be exclusively Liverpool and was probably the type of pattern that Sadler referred to when he said that the painters took one hour to decorate two tiles (see p. 124) Sadler in fact copied some of these borders and used them on his 1757 woodblock tiles (see p. 126). The subjects were interchangeable with a variety of elaborate border designs (pp. 43, 44, 45) and also the octagonal dash border (p. 42). The reclining shepherdess, no. **185,** appears with the octagonal dash border tile no. **194.**
The unusual **"Cherub Border"** is copied from a Dutch design and was also used on woodblock tiles, cf. no. **687,** compare with (Ray, no. 298 and 299).

Liverpool

189. Liverpool.* 1750-70.
12.3 x 0.8 cms. Manganese.

190. Liverpool.** 1750-70.
12.8 x 0.8 cms. Blue.

191. Liverpool.** 1750-70.
12.7 x 0.7 cms. Blue.

192. Liverpool.** 1750-75.
12.9 x 0.9 cms. Pale Blue.
cf. Fig. VII.

193. Liverpool.** 1750-75.
12.7 x 0.7 cms. Pale Blue.

194. Liverpool.** 1750-75.
12.8 x 0.7 cms. Blue.

195. Liverpool.** 1750-75.
12.5 x 0.6 cms. Manganese.

196. Liverpool.** 1750-80.
12.7 x 0.7 cms. Blue.

197. Liverpool.** 1760-80.
12.8 x 0.6 cms. Blue.

198. Liverpool.** 1760-80.
12.5 x 0.6 cms. Blue.

199. Liverpool.** 1780-1800.
13.1 x 0.7 cms. Blue.

200. Liverpool.** 1780-1800.
12.8 x 0.7 cms. Blue.

Fig. VII. Delftware Plate decorated in a pale blue, 23 cm. diameter, 1750-75, Liverpool.** This plate has many of the characteristics found on tiles illustrated on page 42. Compare with no. **192.**

The **"Octagonal Dash" border** is copying a Dutch design but with the addition of dashes. It was predominantly used in Liverpool but was also made at Bristol (cf. Ray, no., 146) and probably London (Ray, 190) (see note on no. **54**). Some of the tiles have marks painted on the back which is a feature of Liverpool. They are:

    No. **195** - the numeral 7 in black. No. **192** - numeral 10 in manganese with a faint number 9 which has been picked up from another tile, which shows that these must have been stacked back to back.

    No. **198** - the numeral 9 in black. No. **200** - the numeral 8 in manganese.

No. **189** is slightly smaller than the other tiles and the border is less heavy (cf. Ray, no. 188). There is a difference in quality between **190** and **191**. No. **194** is the same subject as no. **185**. The shepherd with sheep no. **192** compares with the Liverpool plate, (fig. VII). The well made and finely painted tile no. **193** is in severe contrast to the slapdash of the previous tile and the heavy, thick painting on nos. **194** and **197**. The girl with the rake, no. **197**, is illustrated (cf. Ray, 211) within a floral border, see page 41, as is also no. **199** (Ray, no. 209). Nos. **196** and **200** are typical Liverpool boating scenes and include the usual two swans (cf. Ray, nos. 310 and 307). The girl with the milk churn no. **198** was also used by Sadler on his printed tile no. **706** and was adapted from a design taken from a drawing book by John Bowles dated 1756-7.

201. Liverpool.** 1760-80.
12.5 x 0.6 cms. Blue.

202. Liverpool.** 1780-1800.
13.1 x 0.7 cms. Blue.

No. **201** is an earlier version of **202**. The painting on **202** is very mechanical and the blue has not sunk in. The glaze is very thin and even, and the colour is very white rather like a Dutch early 19th century tile. These observations also apply to nos. **199** and **200**.

Liverpool

203. Liverpool.** 1750-80.
13 x 0.7 cms. Blue.

The tiles on this page and the next all have the **"Louis XV Border"** with variations. John Sadler also used this border on his painted tiles (p. 126). Compare no. **203** with (Ray, no. 292).

204. Liverpool.** 1750-80.
12.7 x 0.7 cms. Dark Blue.

The **'Louis XV Border with feathered corners'** is the rarest design of this group. (cf. Ray, no. 297).

205. Liverpool.** 1750-80.
12.5 x 0.7 cms. Blue.

206. Liverpool.** 1750-80.
12.6 x 0.7 cms. Blue.

The **"Louis XV Border with the buttercup corners"** (cf. Ray, no. 205). The buttercup design was commonly used with oriental figure subjects (p. 57). Note the buttercups on tile no. **205** only have four petals. The subjects on tiles **207** and **208** are known with a variety of surrounds including the floral border (cf. Ray, no. 212 and 207).

207. Liverpool.** 1750-80.
12.6 x 0.7 cms. Blue.

208. Liverpool.** 1750-80.
12.6 x 0.7 cms. Blue.

209. Liverpool.** 1750-80.
12.5 x 0.6 cms. Blue.

210. Liverpool.** 1750-80.
12.5 x 0.6 cms. Blue.

211. Liverpool.** 1750-80.
12.6 x 0.7 cms. Blue.

212. Liverpool.** 1750-80.
12.7 x 0.7 cms. Dark Blue.

213. Liverpool.** 1750-80.
12.5 x 0.7 cms. Very dark Manganese.

214. Liverpool.** 1750-80.
13 x 0.6 cms. Dark Blue.

215. Liverpool.** 1750-80.
12.5 x 0.6 cms. Blue.

216. Liverpool.** 1750-80.
13 x 0.7 cms. Blue.

217. Liverpool.** 1750-80.
12.6 x 0.7 cms. Blue.

These tiles have the **"Louis XV Border with Diaper corners"** but the difference in painting is extreme from the almost royal blue of no. **212** and the dark manganese of no. **213**, to the wishy-washy palette of **209** and **210**. The painting of tiles **209** and **210** is very fine and if they were without a border could be mistaken for the fine quality Bristol or London tiles on page 37. The two Dutchmen skating, no. **217**, is not unlike the painting on two London tiles (cf. Horne, nos. 25 and 26). For London tiles with a diaper corner see page 30.

British?/London/Bristol

218, 219, 220. Possibly British. 1750-70.
12.8 x 0.8 cms. Blue.

Although this style of border is Dutch the painting lacks confidence. The tiles are well made and have a pinky red body with chamfered edges. The glaze has a bluish background but the painting has characteristics of London, Bristol and Liverpool! The accentuated curve at the corners of the octagonal border also appears on the tiles from Pollok House (see fig. I, p. 8). For a Dutch example see Ray, page 91 and for a tile with a similar border found in Bristol see Ray, page 101, figure 30.

221. London.** 1760-90.
12.9 x 0.8 cms. Blue.

222. Bristol.** 1750-70.
13.3 x 0.7 cms. Dark Blue.

223. Bristol.** 1750-70.
13 x 0.9 cms. Manganese.

224. Bristol.** 1750-75.
13.4 x 0.6 cms. Blue.

The pottery kiln with hovels attached on London tile no. **221** is the same scene as on Bristol tile no. **222**. These two tiles are about the same date and this same scene (not illustrated) is known as part of the set of later London tiles shown on page 38. The diaper corners on tile **221** can be compared with those on page 30. Tile no. **222** which is very well made with two pinholes on the back, fits in with the Bristol tiles on page 34. Although the studded border on tile no. **223** was made at Bristol and Liverpool, the delicate painting and flat back to this tile suggests it is Bristol, compare with no. **183**. Tile no. **224** is large, well made and has a flat back, all characteristics of Bristol. Compare the painting of the tree with tile no. **182**.

225. Liverpool. 1760-75.
12.9 x 0.8 cms. Polychrome, Brown, Blue, Orange, Green, Yellow.

226. Liverpool. 1760-75.
12.6 x 0.6 cms. Polychrome, Green, Blue, Orange, Yellow, Manganese.

These attractive scenes are copied from engravings, no. **225** being taken from "The Drawing Book" by John Bowles published in 1756-57. For similar tiles and others from this series (cf. Ray, p. 157).

During the second half of the 18th century, Liverpool created many new designs that had not been inspired by the Dutch.

227. Liverpool. 1750-75.
12.8 x 0.7 cms. Manganese.

228. Liverpool. 1750-75.
12.8 x 0.7 cms. Manganese.

These scenes have been copied from a set of etchings by Nicolaes Berchem. They formed the frontispiece of the book from which the sheep and the goat drawings were taken (cf. p. 52). For copies of the original drawings (cf. Ray, p. 148 figs. 41 and 42).

London/Liverpool

ANIMAL SUBJECTS

229. London.* 1700-30.
12.8 x 1.1 cms. Dark intense Blue.

230. London.** 1725-50.
15 x 0.9 cms. Bright Blue, High Glaze powdered Blue.

231. London.** 1740-60.
12.7 x 0.9 cms. Blue, powdered Blue.

232. London.** 1760-80.
12.7 x 0.7 cms. Blue, powdered Blue.

233. Liverpool.* 1740-60.
Blue, Dark powdered Manganese.

Not many animal subjects were painted at London. A greater number were made at Bristol but the majority came from Liverpool. No. **229** is a rare early example with Barred Ox-head corners. The intensity of the blue and sponged trees are early features, but it is difficult to be certain about attribution although the back is rough which is a London feature. The London tile **230** is a larger version of the tiles on pages 19, 61 and 62 and the same scene appears on a normal sized tile (Ray, no. 321). These large tiles are rare but have been recorded with flower designs (Ray, no. 242 and Horne, p. 20). No. **231** is the same as those on page 62, similar corners having been found at Vauxhall (Britton, p. 71, fig. 12K). **232** is slightly thinner and less bright which suggest a later date and the cow also appears on Dutch tiles. No. **233** is probably Liverpool and can be compared with no. **32**.

234, 235, 236, 237, 238, 239. London. 1740-60.
12.5 x 0.7 cms. Blue.

Tiles **234-239** form a continuous hunting scene which is reminiscent of that found on brown stoneware mugs made in London during the second quarter of the 18th century. The corner motif has been found in London, cf. page 60. The Blacksmiths Arms bowl dated 1749 in the Ashmolean Museum has a continuous hunting scene on the outside which includes a similar beater and dog (cf. Lipski, no. 1123).

240. Bristol.* 1740-60.
13 x 0.8 cms. Blue.

241. Bristol.** 1740-60.
12.8 x 0.7 cms. Blue.

242. Liverpool.** 1750-75.
12.7 x 0.7 cms. Blue, Number 5? in blue on reverse.

The painting on no. **240** is similar to a hog illustrated on the Butcher's bowl dated 1753 (Ray "English Delftware Pottery", Pl. 41), which is definitely London. However the size and flowerhead corner motif suggest this to be a Bristol tile. No. **241** is a typical Bristol landscape scene. Compare the corners on page 33. The Fox and Grapes on **242** is possibly a fable (Ray, no. 329) illustrates a fox stealing a fowl and suggests that this may also be a fable.

243. Liverpool.** 1760-75.
12.6 x 0.7 cms. Manganese. These animals are rare and have been taken directly from the "Ladies Amusement", page 109 which was a major source of inspiration for new designs.

244. Liverpool.** 1760-75.
12.6 x 0.7 cms. approx. Manganese.

245. Bristol.*** 1760-75.
12.9 x 0.6 cms. Manganese with Bianco-sopra-bianco Border. The bianco border decoration is the same as that on tile no. **319** which links this tile and those on page 50 with the Bristol tiles on page 34. (Ray, no. 336 and 337) illustrates other animals from this series which have the same border.

Bristol

246, 247, 248 Bristol.*** 1760-75.
249, 250, 251 13.2 x 0.7 cms.
252, 253, 254
255, 256, 257

Some of these designs may have been adapted from the "Ladies Amusement". The quaint inaccuracies of the animals suggest that the original drawings were done in the 16th century. These animals were also available with a Bianco-soprabianco border, see no. **245** and (Ray Pl. 34).

50

Liverpool/London

The scenes on Nos. **258-263** have been copied from Pl. 111 and 112 of the "Ladies Amusement".

The **"Buttercup Corner"** on nos. **258-261** appears only to have been used at Liverpool and is often found in association with chinoiserie subjects (p. 57). No. **262** is basically the same design but with a polychrome border (cf. Ray, 360-361). The scene on **263** is similar but not so well painted (for others in this series, cf. Ray, Pl. 36). The **"Barbed Medallion"** surround on **263** is typically Liverpool and is more usually associated with bird tiles (page 55).

258, 259, Liverpool.** 1760-75.
260, 261   12.6 x 0.7 cms.

262. Liverpool.** 1760-75.
12.8 x 0.9 cms.

263. Liverpool.** 1760-75.
12.6 x 0.5 cms.

264. London. 1750-70.
12.7 x 0.7 cms.

265. Liverpool.** 1760-80.
12.6 x 0.5 cms.

No. **264** compares with the other landscape tiles on page 37 and has possibly two pinholes on the front.
No. **265** has a similar painting style to tile no. **315** and has two fine pinholes on the front.

Liverpool

266

267

268

269

270

271

272. Liverpool. 1750-75.
13 x 0.7 cms. Manganese. Compare with fig. VIII.

266-271 Liverpool. 1750-75.
12.9 x 0.7 cms. (approx). Blue.

The designs for nos. **266** to **272** are derived from a book of etchings by Nicolaes Berchem 1620-83, and came from the same source as no. **227** and no. **228**, which formed the frontispiece for the book. The tiles are known in manganese and may have also been made in Bristol. For other examples in the same series (cf. Ray, p. 185).

273. Liverpool.** 1750-75.
12.9 x 0.7 cms. Dark Blue. Large AJ in black on the reverse.

Fig. VIII. Nicolaes Berchem "Le Cahier a L'Homme" en six feuilles. "Animalia ad vivum delineata et aqua forti aeri impressa, studio et arte Nicolae Berchemi"
Published: Huquier, Paris (V & A Print Room, no. E-776-1965). Compare with tile no. **272** which is painted on the same scale, being pricked out straight from the print.

274. Liverpool. 1750-75.
12.5 x 0.8 cms. Manganese. The story behind this unusual subject has not been identified.

52

BIRDS

275. Liverpool.** 1750-75.
12.6 x 0.6 cms. Polychrome. Blue, Manganese, Orange, Yellow and Green.

276. Liverpool.** 1750-75.
12.7 x 0.5 cms. Polychrome. Manganese, Orange, Yellow and Green. Blue corners.

277. Liverpool.** 1750-75.
12.6 x 0.6 cms. Polychrome. Manganese, Orange, Yellow and Green. Blue corners.

278. Liverpool.** 1750-75.
12.7 x 0.5 cms. Polychrome. Bright Blue, Dark Manganese, Red, Yellow and Green.

279. Liverpool.* 1750-75.
13.1 x 0.7 cms. Blue.

280. Liverpool.** 1750-75.
12.6 x 0.7 cms. Polychrome. Pale Blue, Dark Manganese, Orange, Yellow and Green.

281. Liverpool.** 1750-75.
12.9 x 0.8 cms. Polychrome. Blue, Manganese and Yellow.

282. Liverpool.** 1750-75.
12.8 x 0.8 cms. (approx). Polychrome. Blue, Manganese and Yellow.

283. Liverpool.** 1750-75.
12.9 x 0.8 cms. Polychrome. Blue, Manganese, Orange and Yellow.

Liverpool produced a large range of bird designs, mainly in polychrome but also in blue and white (**279**). Often these tiles were painted in pairs, left and right (**276** and **277**) presumably to balance in a fireplace. The simple "**Leaf corners**" on **275, 276, 277** are very crude and roughly drawn compared with the rest of the painting and were probably decorated by an apprentice. The bird on no. **275** is very similar to the decoration on a dish in the Bristol Collection (Britton, 19-15). The colouring of **278** is similar to tiles **290, 291** and **292**, and the bird on **280** should be compared with **295**. Nos. **281, 282** and **283** are all related by colour, the butterfly being a rare subject. For other tiles of this type (see Ray, Pl. 43).

Bristol

284. Bristol.*** 1760-75.
13.2 x 0.8 cms. This is a substantial tile with a smooth back and is similar to the animal tiles on page 50, (cf. Ray, Pl. 40).

285. Bristol.*** 1760-75. **286.** Bristol.*** 1760-75. **287.** Bristol.*** 1760-75.
13.3 x 0.7 cms.   13.1 x 0.7 cms.   13.1 x 0.7 cms.

Nos. **285** and **286** have the same bianco border that is found on nos. **245** and **319**. Although **287** has a slightly different border pattern all three fit in with the Bristol tiles on page 34. For similar designs (cf. Ray, Pl. 38-39). (Compare with the Liverpool Bianco-sopra-bianco border on p. 57).

288. Bristol.** 1760-75.
13.3 x 0.7 cms.

289. Bristol.** 1760-75.
13.5 x 0.7 cms.

The quality of the painting on **288** and **289** is very fine. The size and smooth surface of these tiles would suggest they are Bristol.

290. Liverpool.** 1760-75.
12.8 x 0.7 cms.

291. Liverpool.** 1760-75.
12.8 x 0.7 cms.

292. Liverpool.** 1760-75.
12.8 x 0.7 cms.

Note the unusual polychrome flower corners.

293. Liverpool.** 1760-75.
12.8 x 0.6 cms.

294. Liverpool.** 1760-75
12.8 x 0.6 cms.

295. Liverpool.** 1760-75
12.8 x 0.6 cms.

Nos. **293** and **295** have the numerals 8 and 5 respectively, in manganese on the reverse. The **"Trellis Border"** on no. **294** would have made this an expensive tile to produce. For others in the same series, (cf. Ray, Pl. 41). This tile has the numeral 7 and 3 (?) in manganese on the reverse. Ray also illustrates a tighter and neater border which he calls the **"Daisy Chain"** (cf. Ray, no. 413).

296. Liverpool.** 1760-75.
12.7 x 0.7 cms.

297. Liverpool.** 1760-75.
12.7 x 0.7 cms.

298. Liverpool.** 1760-75.
12.7 x 0.7 cms.

This **"Barbed Medallion Border"** was commonly used with polychrome bird tiles. For further examples (cf. Ray, Pl. 42) and on tile, no. **263**.

London/Bristol?

CHINOISERIE SUBJECTS

299. London.* 1720-40.
12.8 x 1.0 cms. Darkish Blue. Worn Surface.

A chinoiserie scene on a tile of this type is rare. The identical subject appears on a plate dated 1727 ("Dated English Delftware"—Lipski, no. 346). Polychrome tiles with similar Kang 'Hsi designs are in the Glaisher Collection (cf. Ray, p. 226) but these have cherub head corners and are probably later. This tile has two pinholes on the front, and is thick with straight cut edges. This same subject has been seen on a later Liverpool tile in the Millie Manheim Collection which had a powdered blue border and dandelion corners similar to no. **55.**

300. London or Bristol. 1725-50.
12.5 x 0.7 cms. Dark Blue. Powdered Manganese.

Another tile of this type is at the Red Lodge, Bristol. Similar lively Chinese figures appear on the so called "Niglett Plate" which is dated 1733 (Lipski, no. 376) and on a bowl ("Bristol Collection"—Britton, 12-17), and is known on numerous other pieces of delft of this period. Ray, (no. 555), illustrates a tile of the same type and there is a similarity between these and the London floral tiles illustrated on page 62 but also compare with tile no. **343** which is probably Bristol.

301. London.** 1750-75.
Blue and Manganese.
This border decoration of marbling with corners painted in the 'cracked ice' design has not previously been recorded on tiles but is sometimes found on London delftware (fig. IX.). Marbling is also found on a pair of exceptionally rare London delftware lioness figures in the Victoria and Albert Museum (illustrated in "Grosvenor House Catalogue", 1976 p. 45).

Fig. IX. A tinglazed plate decorated in blue and manganese, the design in imitation of marble and "cracked ice". 22 cms. diameter. 1750-75. London.** (courtesy of Liverpool Museum).

302. Liverpool.** 1750-75.
12.6 x 0.7 cms. Blue.

303. Liverpool.** 1750-75.
12.6 x 0.7 cms. Blue.

304. Liverpool.** 1750-75.
12.6 x 0.7 cms. Blue.

305. Liverpool.** 1750-75.
12.6 x 0.7 cms. Blue.

This is a distinctive group with "**Buttercup corners**" and were also made in manganese and polychrome. Ray (p. 229), illustrates several more subjects. Some of these tiles are marked on the back. **302**-Numeral 7 in black; **303**-Numeral 7 in manganese; **305**-Horizontal blue line.

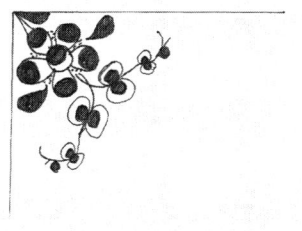

Fig. X. An unusual corner motif on a Liverpool tile at the Red Lodge, Bristol. The scene on this tile is of a Chinese figure similar to no. **306**.

306. Liverpool.** 1750-75.
12.6 x 0.7 cms. Blue

307. Liverpool.** 1750-75.
12.4 x 0.7 cms. Manganese. Bianco-sopra bianco border.

308. Liverpool.** 1750-75.
12.4 x 0.7 cms. Manganese. Bianco-sopra-bianco border

No. **306** has a Buttercup corner which has been incorporated with an unusual border. A similar tile at the Red Lodge, Bristol has another variation to this corner, (see fig. X). The oriental figures on **306, 307** and **308** have all been copied from the "Ladies Amusement," Pl. 57. Nos. **307** and **308** are Liverpool examples of Bianco-sopra-bianco and should be compared with the Bristol equivalents on page 54. For other tiles in this same series see (E.C.C. Vol. 11 Part 2, Pl. 79).

Liverpool

309. Liverpool.** 1750-75.
12.8 x 0.7 cms.

310. Liverpool.** 1750-75.
12.8 x 0.9 cms.

311. Liverpool.** 1750-75.
12.5 x 0.5 cms.

312. Liverpool.** 1750-75.
12.7 x 0.8 cms.

313. Liverpool.** 1750-75.
12.7 x 0.8 cms.

314. Liverpool.** 1750-75.
12.7 x 0.8 cms.

The **"Michaelmas daisy corner"** on nos. **309** and **310** is typical of Liverpool and seems to be only used with oriental scenes. Sometimes this corner is used with a **"Fish Roe Border"**, as seen on nos. **311** to **314**. Note that the border decoration on nos. **313** and **314** has three bands of "fish roe" with smaller daisy corners, compared with only two on nos. **311** and **312**. These figures are interchangeable, no. **310** being almost identical to no. **314** (cf. Ray, Pl. 57 and 58).

315. Liverpool.** 1750-75.
12.7 x 0.6 cms.

Compare the cloud effect of this unusual subject with tile no. **265**. There are two small pinholes on the front and the numeral 155 in manganese on the reverse.

316. Bristol.** 1760-75.
12.7 x 0.8 cms.

317. Bristol.*** 1760-75.
13.2 x 0.7 cms.

318. Bristol.** 1760-75.
13.3 x 0.8 cms.

The border on no. **316** is far less pronounced than on **317** (cf. Ray, no. 579). No. **317** also comes in polychrome and for a plate with a similar design (cf. Ray, fig. 53). This tile has four pinholes on the reverse, whilst **318** has two. The trellis bridge with two birds is an unrecorded tile design but the colouring of the trees should be compared with the tile picture no. **679** on page 122.

319. Bristol.*** 1760-75.
13.3 x 0.7 cms.

Fig. XI. A delftware plate painted with a typical river scene surrounded by a bianco-sopra-bianco border and dated '1761'.
Diameter 22.5 cms. Bristol.***.

Tile no. **319** is painted with a river scene often used by Bristol decorators, see fig. XI. In size and thickness it fits in with the Bristol tiles on p. 34, and the bianco border is the same as on nos. **245, 285** and **286** (for a Liverpool Bianco-sopra-bianco border see p. 57).

FLOWER VASES

320, 321, 322, 323, 324, 325.
London.** 1720-40.
12.6 x 0.9 cms. Polychrome. Blue,
Red and Green.

Very similar patterns were also made in blue and manganese. Garner found fragments of this corner motif at Lambeth (cf. Ray, p. 99 fig. 27). These bright colours were popular on delftware during the 1720's and 30's. Compare with fig. XII and also (cf. Ray, Pl. 52).

Fig. XII. Polychrome (blue, red, green) dish decorated with a vase of flowers. Diameter 33.5 cms., circa 1730, London.**
A similar vase of flowers appears on a blue decorated tankard dated 1728 (Lipski, no. 813). The same scene but much more elaborate was used on the tile panel on page 114.

326, 327, 328, 329, 330. London.** 1730-50.

13 x 0.9 cms. Bright Blue, High glaze.

The earliest use of a carnation head with a powdered manganese background appears on two Grace plates dated 1739 (Lipski, no. 447) and a similar plate (Lipski, no. 446) has an octagonal centre similar to these tiles (powdered blue was not used in Holland). For other related tiles with this same border see pages 19, 23, 48 and 62. Tile no. **326** has unusual corners.

Fig. XIII. This corner motif appears on two tiles in the Victoria & Albert, one with a powdered blue border and the other with powdered green cf. **338,** their centres being painted with a vase of flowers similar to no. **328** but in polychrome.

332. London. 1740-60.

12.7 x 0.9 cms. (Courtesy of Hants Museum Service) (DA 1988/52). Blue. Several tiles of this type have been noted and would have been fixed at an angle.

331. London.** 1730-50.
Bright Blue, High gloss. This tile has a similar vase of flowers to no. **327** but has unusual angel head corners.

333. London.** 1730-50.
13 x 0.8 cms. Blue. Powdered Manganese. Compare with no. **334.**

London

334. London.** 1730-50.
13 x 0.8 cms.

335. London.*** 1730-50.
12.8 x 0.9 cms.

336. London.** 1730-50.
12.7 x 0.8 cms.

337. London.** 1730-50.
12.6 x 0.9 cms.

338. London.** 1730-50.
12.9 x 0.9 cms.

339. London.** 1730-50.
12.6 x 0.8 cms.

340. London.** 1740-60.
12.5 x 0.8 cms.

341. London.** 1740-60.
12.5 x 0.8 cms.

342. London.* 1750-70.
12.5 x 0.7 cms.

All these tiles are similar and compare with those on the preceding page. A tile very like no. **335** but with blue corners and a powdered manganese border was excavated at the Vauxhall Pottery site (Britton, p. 71). It is most unusual to find powdered red no. **337** (cf. no. **47**) and powdered green no. **338**. For others of this type see pages 19, 23, 48 and 61. The cherub corner nos. **337** and **339** are the same as those on tiles **17** and **18**. A very pale powdered manganese has been used on no. **341** which contrasts with the heavy blue painting of the design. The colours of **340** and **342** are not as bright and these may be a little later, (for comparable tiles, see Ray, Pl. 49).

343. Bristol.** 1730-50.
12.0 x 0.8 cms.

344. Possibly London. 1730-50.
12.7 x 0.9 cms.

345. Bristol. 1730-50.
13.3 x 0.8 cms.

No. **343** is more commonly found with blue corners. The glaze is grey, thin and finely pitted similar to nos. **30** and **97**. Lipski says that wasters of similar tiles were found on Bristol pottery sites (cf. Ray, no. 499). The style of painting is very similar to the recess tile no. **664**. Tile no. **344** has the same vase of flowers as no. **343** but has been painted in a different way with unusual carnation corners. No. **345** has a Bristol type glaze but has an unusually shaped central reserve and is larger than the ones Ray illustrates (Pl. 23).

346. London.** 1740-60.
12.8 x 0.9 cms.

347. London.** 1720-40.
12.3 x 0.9 cms.

348. London.** 1740-70.
12.8 x 0.7 cms.

The corner motif nos. **346-348** has been found in London (see p. 60) and an almost identical contemporary chinese porcelain copy of no. **346** is illustrated in (Horne, p. 20). Tile no. **348** has a noticeable "duck egg blue" glaze and may be later than the others. The painting is also very severe. A label on the back of this tile reads "Taken from the wall of a very old butcher's shop demolished in Cambridge in 1925".

349. London.** 1730-50.
12.3 x 0.8 cms.

350. London.** 1740-60.
12.4 x 0.7 cms.

351. London.** 1740-60.
12.4 x 0.7 cms.

No. **349** has a variation on the corner motif and is unusual with flying birds. The polychrome tile no. **350** has a similar "duck egg blue" glaze to no. **348**. No. **351** is a later version of this popular flower vase design.

Liverpool

352. Liverpool.** 1760-75.
12.8 x 0.6 cms. Blue.

353. Liverpool.** 1760-75.
12.8 x 0.6 cms. Blue.

354. Liverpool.** 1750-70.
12.5 x 0.8 cms. Blue.

355. Liverpool.** 1750-70.
12.6 x 0.6 cms. Manganese.

356. Liverpool.** 1750-70.
12.5 x 0.7 cms. Deep Blue.

357. Liverpool.** 1750-70.
12.5 x 0.7 cms. Deep Blue.

358. Liverpool.** 1750-70.
12.8 x 0.8 cms. Manganese.

All these tiles have typical Liverpool borders. The Barred Ox-head corners on **352** and **353** are more usually found with landscape scenes, cf. page 36. The Ragged Flower corners on no. **354** and **355** can be compared with nos. **61-63** although the flower vase on no. **354** is similar to a London design, no. **346**. The Studded Border on no. **356** and **357** has been found at Liverpool (cf. Ray, p. 104 fig. 33) and can be compared with no. **184** (Note this border was also used at Bristol, cf. no. **183**). The Barbed Medallion Border on no. **358** is more commonly associated with bird or animal tiles (pages 51 and 55).

Liverpool/Bristol

359. Liverpool. 1740-60.
12.5 x 0.8 cms. Predominantly Blue with Yellow centres to flowers and the pot in orange-brown.

360. Bristol.*** 1760-75.
13.5 x 0.7 cms. Bianco-sopra-bianco border decoration with a polychrome centre. Blue, Green, Yellow, Manganese and Red.

361. Liverpool.** 1760-75.
12.5 x 0.7 cms. Polychrome. Blue, Green, Yellow, Orange and Manganese.

362. Bristol.** 1760-75.
13.3 x 0.7 cms. Polychrome. Blue, Yellow, Green, Orange and Dark Manganese.

363. Liverpool.** 1760-75.
12.8 x 0.7 cms. Polychrome. Blue, Yellow, Green, Orange and Pale Manganese.

364. Liverpool.** 1760-75.
12.7 x 0.8 cms. Polychrome. Blue, Yellow, Green, Orange and Manganese.

365. Liverpool.* 1750-75.
12.5 x 0.8 cms. Polychrome. Mainly Yellow, Blue, Orange and Manganese.

366. Liverpool.** 1760-75.
12.7 x 0.8 cms. Polychrome. Blue, Green, Yellow, Manganese and Orange.

367. Liverpool.* 1760-75.
12.8 x 0.7 cms. Polychrome. Mainly Yellow, Green, Blue and Manganese.

No. **359** is possibly representing an auricula and is painted in a very simple way. The pattern is unrecorded but the glaze would suggest this to be Liverpool. No. **360** is a typical Bristol tile with three pinholes on the back and compares with the tiles on page 34. No. **361** is a Liverpool interpretation of a similar basket of flowers. Tiles no. **361, 363, 364** and **366** are all painted in the typical Liverpool "Fazackerly" colours, whereas **365** and **367** are slightly different. The larger tile, no. **362** is a Bristol interpretation of Liverpool tile no. **363**, note that the Liverpool tiles have a much whiter background, no. **366** is a rare illustration of a delftware bowl being used with a flower display. For other tiles of this type, see (Ray, Pl. 53).

Liverpool/Bristol

368. Liverpool. 1750-75.
12.5 x 0.7 cms. Manganese.

369. Liverpool or Bristol. 1750-75.
12.5 x 0.7 cms. Blue.

370. Liverpool.* 1770-85.
12.7 x 0.8 cms. Blue.

These three tiles are all unusual. The painting on no. **368** is clearly executed and this may be Liverpool but the corner motif is unrecorded. The corners on no. **369** are a type of Michaelmas Daisy but is different to those on page 58 and the glaze is rather thin and dry. No. **370** is well made with a fairly smooth back, the corners are unusual but there are traces of green enamel on the back which is normally associated with the Liverpool transfer printed tiles.

371. Liverpool. 1750-75.
13 x 0.7 cms. Dark Blue.

372. Bristol.** 1760-75.
13.2 x 0.7 cms. Dark Blue.

373. Liverpool. 1790-1800.
13.5 x 0.6 cms. Bright Blue.

No. **371** is different to the London flower vases on page 63, the corners being close to **375**. The design on no. **372** is unknown but is the same as that on **373** although this is painted in a completely different style. No. **372** is a well made tile in the Bristol manner with four pinholes on the back. No. **373** is large and thin, and painted in a bright blue which suggests it was made at a late date.

Liverpool/Bristol

FLOWERS

374. Liverpool. 1760-80.
13.1 x 0.65 cms. Dark Blue.

375. Liverpool. 1760-80.
13.2 x 0.7 cms. Dark Blue.

376. Liverpool. 1760-80.
12.9 x 0.8 cms. Blue.

These three tiles are different in size, thickness, colour and glaze and show quite different interpretations of the same design. Whilst they might all be from Liverpool, other places of production should also be considered (perhaps Ireland!). The glaze is missing from the top edge of no. **374** which suggests it is a second. No. **375** has a very blue glaze and the interpretation of the stylized plant corner motif is small and tight. No. **376** has a whiter glaze and the painting is less precise.

377. Liverpool.** 1760-80.
12.6 x 0.5 cms. Polychrome.

378. Liverpool.* 1760-80.
12.5 x 0.7 cms. Dark Manganese.

379. Liverpool.* 1760-80.
12.6 x 0.7 cms. Blue.

No. **377** is typical of many simple flower motifs that were produced at Liverpool at this time, the thinness of no. **377** suggesting a late date. This tile has the numeral 4 in manganese on the reverse and Ray (p. 207) illustrates other similar tiles. No. **378** is also a typical Liverpool tile, although Ray illustrates a similar design (cf. no. 468), which could be Bristol and compares another similar flower motif (Ray, no. 472), which he suggests could be Lambeth. The simple flower subject on no. **379** is similar to known Liverpool designs (cf. Ray, Pl. 44) although the **"Posy corner"** is unrecorded.

380. Liverpool.* 1780-1800.
128 x 0.7 cms. Vivid Bright Blue.

381. Bristol.* 1760-80.
13.2 x 0.7 cms. Blue.

382. Liverpool. 1780-1800.
12.8 x 0.5 cms. Blue.

The corner motif on no. **380** is very unusual, and the bright blue on a white background suggests a late date. (Ray, no. 435) illustrates a similar tile which is a palish blue. No. **381** is a well made tile, which has three large pin holes on the reverse suggesting Bristol. The design and corners on no. **381** and **382** are unrecorded.

383. London.* 1740-60.
12.6 x 0.65 cms. Blue with powdered Manganese.

384. Liverpool.** 1760-80.
12.6 x 0.7 cms. Blue with powdered Manganese.

385. Liverpool.** 1760-80.
12.6 x 0.6 cms. Manganese.

No. **383** is an unrecorded design but the rough back, shiny glaze and two rather obvious pinholes on the front suggest this to be a London tile. (The same design is known with a vase of flowers). No. **384** is also a very unusual design but has the typical Liverpool numeral on the reverse, '8' in manganese (cf. Ray, no. 443). The studded border on no. **385** was rarely used with flower designs but compare with nos. **356-357** (cf. Ray, no. 441).

386. Liverpool.** 1750-70.
12.6 x 0.7 cms. Blue.

387. London. 1750-70.
12.7 x 0.7 cms. Blue.

388. Liverpool.* 1750-70.
12.9 x 0.7 cms. Blue.

No. **386** has a Liverpool border (see p. 25) and the decoration is the same as on a plate at Williamsburg (1978-216, 1-2). No. **387** may be London but the design is unrecorded, the nearest parallel being in Ray, plate 48. It seems probable that the pattern on no. **388** was made in both Bristol and Liverpool (cf. Ray, no. 442). A fragment of this design was found at the Gilbody site in Liverpool in 1966.

389. Bristol.*** 1750-70.
13.2 x 0.7 cms. Blue.

390. Liverpool.** 1775-1800.
12.8 x 0.6 cms. Manganese and Green.

391. Liverpool.** 1775-1800.
12.7 x 0.7 cms. Manganese and Green.

No. **389** is certainly a Bristol tile being of large size and having four pinholes on the back. The same bunch of grapes design is also found on a Bristol tile with a Bianco-sopra-bianco border (cf. Ray, no. 529 and 530). The corners are unusual. The extensive use of green in the decoration of nos. **390** and **391** was fashionable during the last quarter of the 18th century and the strawberry pattern was often used on "pearlware" pottery decorated in "Pratt" colours.

VINES

392. Liverpool.* 1760-80.
12.8 x 0.7 cms. (approx). Dark Blue.

393. London. 1760-80.
12.5 x 0.8 cms. Polychrome, Manganese, grey Blue and Green.

394. Liverpool. 1760-80.
13.1 x 0.7 cms. Dark Blue.

These designs are all parts of continuous vertical strip patterns which would have been painted as a "right hand" and a "left hand" vine. Two tiles of the same pattern as **392** are illustrated in (Horne, no. 125-126). The pattern on no. **393** peters out being the top end of the decoration and there are signs of three pinholes on the front. The glaze is rather pitted and the green leaves are quite a different colour to tiles no. **395** and **401**. Two more tiles from this series are illustrated in (Ray, nos. 533 and 534) which came from a house in Worcester. No. **392** is finely painted with a clematis vine; the glaze is thin and even and the blue has not sunk in.

Nos. **395** and **396** are rather similar although no. **395** has small diagonally opposite pinholes on the front of each tile. The whitish background on these and the predominant use of green on no. **396** suggests a late date of manufacture.

395. Liverpool.** 1770-90.
12.8 x 0.6 cms. Dark Blue.

396. Liverpool.** 1775-1800.
12.8 x 0.7 cms. Green and Manganese.

London/Bristol/Liverpool

EDGING TILES

397   398   399   400   401

397. London.** 1750-70.
6.4 x 0.7 cms. Manganese.

398. London.*** 1750-70.
6.3 x 0.7 cms. Dark Blue.

399. London.** 1740-60.
6.3 x 0.7 cms. Manganese.

400. London.* 1750-70.
6.5 x 0.8 cms. Blue.

401. Bristol.** 1760-70.
6.8 x 0.6 cms. Polychrome.

EDGING TILES are rare survivors and have tended to be thrown away when fireplaces etc. have been removed. They are usually half the width of a full size tile but quarter width tiles are also known (E.C.C. Vol 9 Part 1 1973, Pl. 60).
The only panel known with it's original border is the "Cock and Bottle" tavern sign (Britton, p. 178). This also includes "quarter" tiles which are extremely rare.
Except in the case of the geometric designs, two tiles are required to complete a pattern see nos. **402** and **403** and for further examples see (Ray, p. 237). For a printed border tile see page 132.
No. **397** has two pinholes on the front and is also known in blue. No. **398** has been found at Vauxhall (E.C.C. Vol 9 Part 2 1973, Pl. 136) and is close to a Dutch design. No. **399** also has two pinholes on the front and this Greek Key pattern is recorded in blue (cf. Horne, p. 21). The rough back of no. **400** suggests this might be London. The large size of no. **401** and colouring, which is close to tile no. **318** suggest this is Bristol. No. **402** is painted in a heavy bright blue on a duck egg ground which is often found on later London delftware whereas no. **403** is a much softer blue that has tended to "sink in", which is typical of Liverpool.

402   403

402. London.** 1760-80.
6.2 x 0.8 cms. Dark Blue.

403. Liverpool.** 1760-80.
6.3 x 0.7 cms. Blue.

404. Liverpool.* 1750-75.
12.5 x 0.7 cms. Blue.

405. Liverpool.* 1750-75.
12.5 x 0.7 cms. Blue. These appear to be Liverpool, although both these designs are rare (cf. Ray, no. 470).

Liverpool/London

STYLIZED FLOWERS AND PATTERNS

406. Liverpool.** 1750-75.
12.7 x 0.7 cms. Blue.

407. Liverpool.* 1750-75.
12.0 x 0.8 cms. Dark Blue with red centre.

These tiles show quite different interpretations of the same design and therefore several factories must also be considered.

No. **406** is a typical Liverpool tile, (cf. Ray, no. 539). Even allowing for no. **407** being slightly cut down, this is a small tile. The glaze is rather white and pitted and the back is fairly rough like a London tile although the corner is similar to other Liverpool examples. cf. no. **168**.

The corners on no. **408** have been painted in a clumsy fashion compared with the more delicate centre which suggests two hands decorated this tile. The same tile but with different corners is illustrated in (Ray, no. 541).

Although no. **409** is similar to the previous tile it is brighter and clearer, the body is flat and thin and mechanically made.

No. **410** has all the characteristics of Liverpool although Ray illustrates a similar but larger tile in polychrome that is more likely to be Bristol. (cf. Ray no. 543). The border is very similar to that used on the chinoiserie tiles in the Fitzwilliam Museum (Ray, Pl. 56).

No. **411** is a large and well made tile although the painting is clumsy and there is a sign of a pinhole on the front which is not a Bristol feature. Note how the cherubs are not in the corners.

No. **412** is a clean and well painted tile. The two pinholes on the front and the shiny glaze suggest this might be London.

No. **413** has the unusually large cherub heads. The border should be compared the Louis XV border on page 44. For other Angel Head corners see pages 19, 26, 62, 82, 110 and 112.

408. Liverpool.* 1760-90.
12.6 x 0.7 cms. Dark Blue.

409. Liverpool.* 1780-1800.
12.8 x 0.6 cms. Blue.

410. Liverpool.** 1750-75.
12.6 x 0.7 cms. Dark Blue.

411. Liverpool. 1750-75.
13.2 x 0.7 cms. Blue with powdered border.

412. London.* 1750-75.
12.5 x 0.7 cms. Blue with powdered border.

413. Liverpool.** 1750-75.
12.7 x 0.6 cms. Blue.

Liverpool/Bristol/Glasgow

414. Liverpool.* 1750-70.
12.8 x 0.7 cms. Blue.

415. Liverpool.* 1750-70.
13 x 0.8 cms. Blue. (Courtesy of Liverpool Museum).

416. Liverpool.** 1750-70.
12.7 x 0.7 cms. Blue.

417. Bristol.** 1750-70.
13.4 x 0.7 cms. Blue.

418. Liverpool.* 1750-70.
12.6 x 0.6 cms. Blue.

No. **414** is copying a well known Dutch pattern made at Rotterdam circa 1700. Ray (nos. 546, 547 and 548) illustrates other designs similar to **415** that have been copied from a similar source.

No. **416** shows a stylized perfume burner (Ray 545).

No. **417** is large with three pinholes on the back.

No. **418** has the same pattern but is undoubtedly from a different factory. It has two pinholes on the front and the blue has "sunk" in much more (cf. Ray, no. 537) for a version in manganese. The Victoria & Albert Museum have the same pattern in polychrome.

No. **419** is painted with a rococo design which includes a flying dragon. (cf. Ray, no. 538).

No. **420** is smaller and less well drawn. This is another instance of more than one factory using the same design.

419. Bristol.* 1750-70.
13.3 x 0.8 cms. Blue. Manganese diaper.

420. Liverpool.* 1750-70.
12.8 x 0.7 cms. Blue.

421. Glasgow. 1750-70.
(Courtesy of The People's Palace, Glasgow).
This unusual tile was found with no. **24** in the grounds of Glenarbuck House, Glasgow. Although discovered with other tiles that are likely to be Liverpool, this design is unrecorded.
See notes on page 7.

422. London.** 1750-70.
12.3 x 0.8 cms. Blue. (Courtesy of Hants Museum Services, DA1979-75/64).

423. London. 1760-80.
12.7 x 0.6 cms. Polychrome, Blue, Green, Yellow and Manganese.

424. Possibly Bristol. 1750-70.
12.8 x 0.7 cms. Dark Blue.

The **"Quarter Rose corner"** motif would appear to have been used at London and Bristol. Garner recovered fragments of tile no. **422** from Lambeth (Ray, p. 99 fig. 27E). An unglazed waster (see fig. XIV), was recovered from Temple Back, Bristol in 1974. The large corners on no. **423** should be compared with (Ray, no. 35 and fig. 38 p. 128). Ray, (no. 588) illustrates, a polychrome version of no. **424** which he tentatively attributes to Bristol.

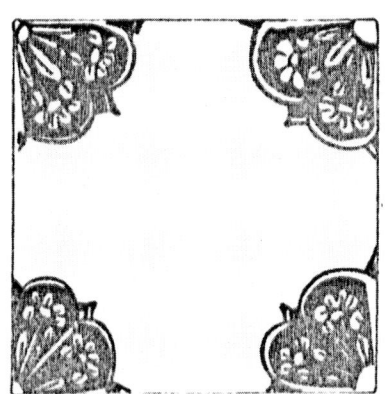  

Fig. XIV. This is the only tile (12 x 0.8 cms.) recovered at Temple Back, Bristol during the excavations of 1974. It was found in three fragments and may possibly be from more than one tile. The tile was a waster and had not been re-fired after decoration.
(Reproduced with kind permission of Bristol Museum).

425. London.** 1750-75.
13 x 0.8 cms. Blue.

426. Liverpool. 1750-75.
12.8 x 0.7 cms. Blue.

The central motif on **425** is Japanese and called 'mon'. This pattern was also used on delft plates (Fig. III page 24) and on the recess tile no. **666**. The tile has two pinholes on the front which suggests London. For a polychrome example (cf. Ray, no. 590). No. **426** is an unrecorded pattern and has been painted in a soft blue.

427. London.* 1770-90.
12.6 x 0.7 cms. Dark Blue.

428. Liverpool.** 1780-1800.
12.8 x 0.7 cms. Blue.

No. **427** has an unrecorded **"Multiple Dash border"**. The strong dark blue and the unevenness of the tile suggest a London manufacture. The central snowflake on no. **428** was also used as an all over pattern and Ray (no. 593), shows the same but with swags which is a late feature. This tile is very white and evenly made and compares with no. **202**.

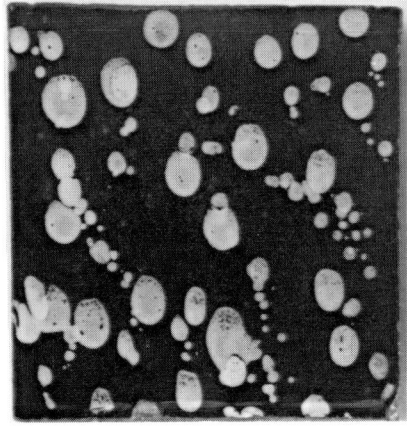

429. London.** 1690-1710.
12.7 x 0.8 cms. Blue with a high gloss.

430. Wincanton.*** 1730-50.
12.8 x 0.7 cms. Blue.

431. Liverpool.** 1770-90.
12.9 x 0.6 cms. Black.

No. **429** is decorated in the style of Nevers faience. Fragments of this type of ware have been found at Norfolk House, Lambeth (cf. Britton, p. 135 no. 98).

The pattern on no. **430** was also made in green, an example of which is in the Birmingham City Art Gallery. The latter is labelled "from Ireson's house in Wincanton". Fragments of similar tiles have also been found at the Wincanton site. (See notes on page 6).

On no. **431** each square has been outlined and then carefully painted over in black. Ray (no. 576), illustrates a similar tile but without the diagonal lines.

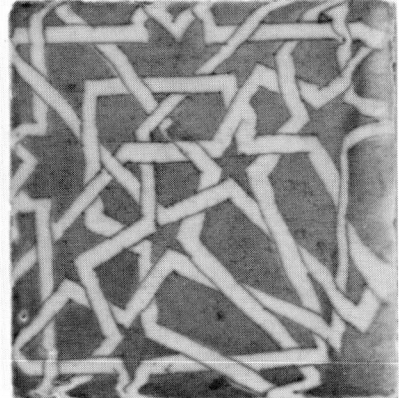

432. London.** 1750-70.
12.7 x 0.8 cms. Blue.

433. London.** 1740-60.
12.7 x 0.7 cms. Manganese and Blue.

434. London.** 1750-70.
13 x 0.9 cms. Manganese and Blue.

The entwined trellis design on no. **432** must have been very difficult to execute which is perhaps why this pattern is rare. There are two pinholes on the front. (See Back Cover).

No. **433** is a fairly rare design which must have been very effective en masse. This has all the characteristics of a London tile with two pinholes on the front. Similar tiles with different scenes are illustrated in (Ray, no. 576 and Horne no. 113).

Denis Cockell found a fragment of no. **434** amongst kiln waste at the Vauxhall pottery in London (E.C.C. Vol. 9 Part 2, 1974 Pl. 136) and the thick glaze with two pinholes on the front is also evidence for these being London. Ray (no. 594), illustrates a similar tile which is tentatively attributed to Bristol as a fragment with a similar design was excavated by Pountney on the Redcliff site.

BIBLICAL TILES

It is very unusual to find religious scenes depicted on English delftware except in the case of tiles where Old and New Testament subjects were produced in profusion. Dutch religious tiles were made in large quantities and had acquired a substantial part of the market. It was from these that the decorators copied many of their designs, of which over 130 English religious subjects have now been recorded, which is still a long way from the 500 plus biblical scenes that have been listed on Dutch tiles (Tegelmuseum 1972 Catalogue, Otterlo Holland).
Often the origin of the designs were taken from engravings, as in "Samson carrying the doors of Gaza" no. **498** where an English tile is copying a Dutch tile, the scene having been taken from Plate 9 of "De Schriftuurlyke Geschiedenissen en Gelyhenissen van het Oude en Nieuwe Verbond" (Amsterdam 1712) (see "Dutch Tiles" Philadelphia Museum of Art, p. 117 Fig. 39). In most cases the designs were adapted and a certain amount of symbolism was used to make the subject more understandable; for instance Christ is nearly always shown with a halo no. **605**, a wealthy or important man such as Isaac, no. **457** is shown wearing a big hat, whilst a king has a crown, no. **514.** Indoor subjects often show tiled floors and have diamond lattice windows which seem to hang suspended in the air, no. **472**. The final result was not always accurate as is shown in no. **525**, Elisha was mocked for having no hair but here the painter has not understood the story. In most cases the London and Bristol potters used the same subjects, either copying each other or using the same Dutch source. There seems to be a far greater profusion of London tiles but with little variety, mostly painted with the Barred Ox-head corners, whereas Liverpool used designs that are often quite different in style.

Additional religious subjects not illustrated in this catalogue are:
    The Ark of the Covenant: Genesis 9 v. 13 (Ray, no. 25) (Bristol Museum).
    The Tower of Babel: Genesis 11 v. 4 (Ray, no. 26).
    The Angel smiting the camp of Sennacherib: Kings 19 v. 35 (Ray, no. 56) (Salisbury Museum).
    The Children of Israel in the Fiery Furnace: Daniel 3 v. 25 (Ray, no. 58) (Salisbury Museum).
    Christ Rising from the Dead: Matthew 28 v. 2 (Ray, no. 94).

London/Bristol/Liverpool

OLD TESTAMENT

TEMPTATION AND FALL: Genesis 3 v. 6

435. London.** 1690-1720.
13 x 0.8 cms. Brightish blue on pinky white ground. The pink appearance of the glaze would suggest London.

436. London.** 1720-50.
12.8 x 0.8 cms. Blue. This scene includes a lion and lioness. A London tile in (Horne, no. 61) has a lion, 2 rabbits and a squirrel. A tile in the V & A has the same scene with a single lion painted in a roundel with cherub corners and is also probably London.

437. Bristol.** 1720-50.
12.9 x 0.7 cms. Strong blue. Ray illustrates several tiles which have this flowerhead corner and have been painted in the same rather sketchy way, (cf. Ray no. 24 & 26).

438. Bristol.** 1720-50.
13 x 0.8 cms. Blue.

439. Liverpool.** 1750-70.
12.5 x 0.7 cms. Blue.

440. Liverpool.** 1750-70.
12.7 x 0.7 cms. Blue.

"AND THEN THEY WERE NAKED":
Genesis 3 v. 7

441. London.** 1740-60.
12.8 x 0.7 cms. Manganese.

THE EXPULSION:
Genesis 3 v. 24

442. London.** 1740-60.
12.8 x 0.7 cms. Manganese.

London/Bristol/Liverpool

CAIN SLAYING ABEL: Genesis 4 v. 4

443. London.** 1740-60.
12.7 x 0.7 cms. (cut down). Blue. For a Liverpool version (cf. Ray, no. 21).

"TWO OF EVERY SORT SHALT THOU BRING INTO THE ARK": Genesis 6 v. 19

444. London.** 1740-60.
12.5 x 0.7 cms. Blue.

THE FLOOD: Genesis 7 v. 19

445. Bristol.*** 1750-70.
12.8 x 0.7 cms. Manganese. (cf. Ray, no. 24).

446. Liverpool.** 1750-75.
12.8 x 0.7 cms. Manganese. (cf. Ray, no. 22).

447. Liverpool.** 1750-75.
12.5 x 0.7 cms. Blue. (cf. Ray, no. 23).

THE BUILDING OF THE TOWER OF BABEL: Genesis 11

448. London.** 1740-60.
12.9 x 0.7 cms. Manganese.

London/Liverpool/Bristol

LOT'S DAUGHTERS MADE THEIR FATHER DRINK WINE: Genesis 19 v. 33

449. London.** 1750-70.
12.5 x 0.6 cms. Blue.

ABRAHAM DISMISSING HAGAR: Genesis 21 v. 14

450. London.* 1730-50.
12.7 x 0.8 cms. Blue. (Courtesy of Hants Museum Service Ref. DA 1985-98/1).

451. London.** 1750-70.
12.7 x 0.8 cms. Blue. (cf. Ray, no. 28) for this scene in reverse.

HAGAR AND ISHMAEL: Genesis 21 v. 14   HAGAR AND THE ANGEL: Genesis 21 v. 15-17

452. Liverpool.** 1740-60.
Light Blue.

453. London.** 1740-70.
12.7 x 0.8 cms. Blue. For this in reverse see (Horne, no. 64).

LOT AND HIS DAUGHTERS: Genesis 24 v. 14

454. London.** 1700-30.
12.7 x 0.8 cms. Blue with a dark blue outline.

455. London.* 1730-50.
13 x 0.8 cms. Manganese. Unusual corners.

456. Bristol.** 1720-50.
13.3 x 0.8 cms. Blue.

London/Liverpool/Bristol

ABRAHAM AND ISAAC: Genesis 22 v. 6

457. London.* 1720-50.
12.8 x 0.8 cms. Blue.

458. Bristol.** 1720-50.
13 x 0.8 cms. Blue. cf. Ray, no. 29.

459. Liverpool.** 1750-70.
12.5 x 0.7 cms. Blue. cf. **517**.

THE SACRIFICE OF ISAAC: Genesis 22 v. 9-12

460. London.** 1720-50.
12.6 x 0.7 cms. Blue.

461. London.** 1740-60.
12.6 x 0.6 cms. Blue.

ELIEZER OFFERS JEWELS TO REBECCA AT THE WELL: Genesis 24 v. 45

462. London.* 1700-20.
12.9 x 0.9 cms. Blue.

463. London.** 1740-60.
12.9 x 0.7 cms. Manganese.

JACOB GIVES ESAU A MESS OF POTTAGE: Genesis 25 v. 27-34

ESAU COMING TO ISAAC ON HIS DEATHBED: Genesis 27 v. 25

 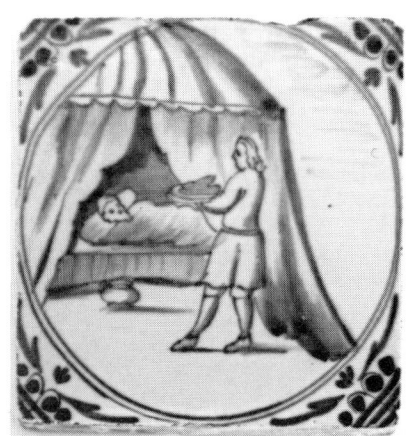

464. London.* 1740-60.
12.4 x 0.9 cms. Manganese. Unusual corners.

465. London.** 1740-60.
12.6 x 0.8 cms. Blue. Unusual corners.

London

JACOB'S LADDER: Genesis 28 v. 12

466. London.** 1730-60.
12.7 x 0.7 cms. Blue. For a Bristol version see Ray, no. 31.

JACOB AND RACHEL AT THE WELL: Genesis 29 v. 10

467. London.** 1760-80.
12.8 x 0.7 cms. Blue. For the same subject without a border (cf. Ray, p. 30). Not to be confused with no. **462** Rebecca at the well or no. **612** Jesus with the Woman of Samaria.

Fig. XV. A delftware tea caddy decorated in blue with the scene of Jacob and Rachel at the well.
Height 8.8 x 6.2 x 8.3 cms. Circa 1710. London.**
A very similar silver tea caddy in the Victoria and Albert Museum is dated 1709.
For the reverse side see fig. XVII on page 95.

JACOB WRESTLING WITH AN ANGEL: Genesis 33 v. 24

468. London.* 1720-50.
12.8 x 0.8 cms. Blue. cf. Ray, no. 32.
A fragment of this subject was found at Lambeth (Ray, fig. 23 p. 98). The same scene but in reverse is on a tile in the V & A which is probably Liverpool having cherub corners similar to Ray, no. 94.

469. London.* 1730-50.
12.8 x 0.8 cms. Blue. This is a different version of the same subject.

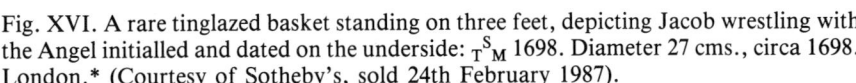

Fig. XVI. A rare tinglazed basket standing on three feet, depicting Jacob wrestling with the Angel initialled and dated on the underside: $_T{}^S{}_M$ 1698. Diameter 27 cms., circa 1698. London.* (Courtesy of Sotheby's, sold 24th February 1987).
Several baskets of this type have been recorded and were probably made in London (E.C.C. Vol. 13 Part 2 1988, "Some Delftware Baskets"—Cockell p. 121). This early date shows that this well known tile subject was being produced in London during the 17th century.

JOSEPH PUT INTO A PIT: Genesis 27 v. 24

470. London.* 1760-80.
12.5 x 0.7 cms. Blue. For the same subject in reverse (cf. Ray, no. 33).

JOSEPH'S COAT BROUGHT TO ISRAEL: Genesis 37 v. 33

471. London.* 1720-50.
12.6 x 0.8 cms. Manganese. Painted in reverse to **472**.

472. Bristol.** 1720-50.
13 x 0.8 cms. Very dark Mauve. Precise and clear, cf. no. **510**.

473. Liverpool.* 1750-70.
12.7 x 0.7 cms. Blue. An inferior tile which has not been fully painted.

JOSEPH AND POTIPHAR'S WIFE: Genesis 39 v. 12

474. London.* Possibly circa 1680.
12.4 x 0.8 cms. Light blue. Compare with the Popish Plot tiles (Ray, nos. 17 & 19) which have similar unusual corners. They are also the same size and have had trouble with the glaze running (see page 17) cf. no. **598**.

475. London.** 1740-60.
12.6 x 0.8 cms. Blue.

476. Bristol.** 1720-50.
13 x 0.8 cms. Blue.

JOSEPH INTERPRETING THE BUTLER AND BAKER'S DREAMS: Genesis 40 v. 8

477. London.* 1720-50.
12.9 x 0.9 cms. Blue. Ray, no. 36, illustrates the scene in reverse. The V & A have a London tile with this subject within a powdered manganese border with Quarter Rosette corners.

MOSES DISCOVERED BY THE PHAROAH'S DAUGHTER: Exodus 2 v. 5

478. London.** 1750-70.
12.5 x 0.7 cms. Blue.

MOSES RECEIVING THE TABLETS OF THE LAW: Deuteronomy 5 v. 22

479. London.** 1760-80.
12.2 x 0.7 cms. Dark Blue.

480. Bristol.** 1720-50.
13 x 0.7 cms. Blue. Similar to (Ray, no. 37).

481. Liverpool.* 1750-70.
12.8 x 0.8 cms. Blue. cf. Ray, no. 38. The Cherub corners are unusual.

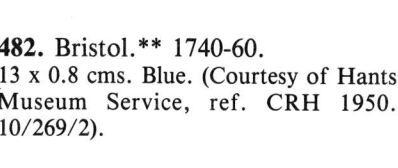

482. Bristol.** 1740-60.
13 x 0.8 cms. Blue. (Courtesy of Hants Museum Service, ref. CRH 1950. 10/269/2).

MOSES AND THE BURNING BUSH: Exodus 3-4

483. London.* 1720-50.
13 x 0.9 cms. Manganese. Moses is shown with his shoes off because he is standing on holy ground.

484. London.** 1740-60.
12.3 x 0.9 cms. Blue. cf. page 23.

485. London.** 1710-30.
12.8 x 0.7 cms. Dark Blue. cf. no. **65.**

THE GATHERING OF MANNA: Exodus 16 v. 11-36

486. London.** 1730-50.
12.3 x 0.8 cms. Blue.

487. London. 1750-70.
12.7 x 0.8 cms. Manganese. Unusual with a halo.

488. London.** 1740-60.
12.8 x 0.8 cms. Powder Blue Border. Moses is sometimes depicted with horns.

MOSES STRIKES WATER FROM A ROCK: Exodus 17 v. 6

489. Liverpool.** 1750-80.
12.6 x 0.7 cms. Blue. (cf. Ray, 39).

MOSES AND THE BRAZEN SERPENT: Numbers 21 v. 9

490. Liverpool.** 1750-70.
12.6 x 0.7 cms. Blue. (cf. Ray, no. 40).

A SPY RETURNING FROM CANAAN: Numbers 13 v. 23

491. Liverpool.** 1760-80.
12.8 x 0.7 cms. Blue.

London

BALLAAM AND THE ASS: Numbers 22 v. 27

492. London.* 1720-50.
13 x 0.8 cms. Shiny Blue. (cf. Ray, no. 41).

RAHAB HELPING THE SPIES TO ESCAPE: Joshua 2 v. 15

493. London.** 1760-80.
12.7 x 0.8 cms. Blue. Similar to (Ray, no. 42). cf. Horne, no. 66 for same in reverse.

THE SETTING UP OF A MONUMENT FOR THE PRESERVATION OF THE ARK OF THE COVENANT: Joshua 4

494. London.* 1710-40.
12.4 x 0.8 cms. Blue.

JAEL KILLING SISERA: Judges 4 v. 21

495. London.* 1730-50.
12.8 x 0.7 cms. Manganese. (cf. Ray 43).

London/Liverpool

GIDEON'S FLEECE: Judges 6 v. 36-40

496. London.** 1730-50.
12.9 x 0.8 cms. Manganese.

JEPHTHAH SETTING OUT AGAINST THE CHILDREN OF AMMON: Judges 11 v. 32

497. London.** 1740-60.
13 x 0.8 cms. Manganese.

SAMSON CARRYING OFF THE GATES OF GAZA: Judges 16 v. 3

498. Liverpool.** 1740-60.
12.5 x 0.6 cms. Blue. (cf. Ray, no. 44).

499. Liverpool.** 1740-60.
12.7 x 0.7 cms. Blue.

500. Liverpool.** 1750-70.
12.7 x 0.8 cms. Blue. cf. page 39.

SAMSON KILLING THE LION: Judges 14

501. London.** 1730-50.
12.7 x 0.8 cms. Blue.

502. London.** 1730-50.
12.8 x 0.7 cms. Manganese.

THE SHEARING OF SAMSON: Judges 16 v. 19

503. London.** 1720-50.
12.6 x 0.9 cms. Shiny Blue.

504. Bristol.** 1740-60.
13.3 x 0.8 cms. Manganese. (cf. Ray, no. 45) for this subject in reverse.

505. Liverpool.** 1750-70.
12.7 x 0.7 cms. Blue.

RUTH AND BOAZ: Ruth 3 v. 7

506. London.** 1700-20.
12 x 0.8 cms. Hard Blue high gloss. Unusually small this tile relates to a series painted with typical landscape scenes, illustrated in Horne (nos. 4-8). Compare with **74, 540** and **622**.

SAUL GOING WITH SERVANT TO SEEK THE ASSES: 1 Samuel 9 v. 3

507. Liverpool.** 1750-70.
12.8 x 0.7 cms. Blue. Compare the style of painting on page 39.

SAMUEL ANOINTING SAUL: 1 Samuel 10

508. London.** 1700-30.
12.9 x 0.9 cms. Dark Blue.

London/Bristol/Liverpool

GOLIATH SETTING OUT TO CHALLENGE THE ISRAELITES: 1 Samuel 17 v. 48

509. London.** 1740-60.
12.8 x 0.7 cms. Manganese.

DAVID BEHEADING GOLIATH: 1 Samuel 17 v. 51

510. Bristol.** 1720-50.
13 x 0.7 cms. Very dark Mauve. A good quality tile which is from the same set as no. **472.** (cf. Ray, no. 47) for this subject in reverse.

511. Liverpool.** 1740-60.
12.8 x 0.7 cms. Blue.

DAVID RETURNING WITH GOLIATH'S HEAD: 1 Samuel 17 v. 54

512. London.** 1700-30.
12.9 x 0.8 cms. Blue. For a slightly later tile (cf. Ray, no. 48), and for a different version see (Britton, no. 223 p. 184).

THE WITCH OF ENDOR CALLING UP SAMUEL BEFORE KING SAUL: 1 Samuel 28

513. London.** 1730-50.
12.8 x 0.8 cms. Manganese.

London/Liverpool

KING DAVID COVETS BATHSHEBA: 2 Samuel 11 v. 2-17

514. London.* 1700-20.
13.2 x 0.8 cms. Bright blue. Similar style to page 26.

AHITOPHEL HANGS HIMSELF: 2 Samuel 17 v. 23

515. Liverpool.** 1750-80.
12.8 x 0.6 cms. Blue.

JOAB SLAIN AT THE HORNS OF THE ALTAR: 1 Kings 2 v. 28

516. London.** 1750-80.
12.5 x 0.7 cms. Blue. This scene in manganese was found at Vauxhall by Denis Cockell (E.C.C. Vol. 99 Part 2 1974, Pl. 135).

517. Liverpool.** 1750-70.
12.8 x 0.8 cms. approx. Blue. Compare with nos. **459** and **545**.

KING SOLOMON PRAYING TO GOD TO BLESS THE TEMPLE: 1 Kings 8

518. London.** 1740-60.
Manganese.

London/Bristol

THE DISOBEDIENT PROPHET: 1 Kings 13 v. 24

519. London.* 1720-50.
12.7 x 0.8 cms. Blue. (cf. Ray, no. 49).

520. London.** 1750-70.
12.7 x 0.7 cms. Blue with dark powdered blue.

ELIJAH FED BY THE RAVENS: 1 Kings 17 v. 5

521. London.** 1740-60.
12.8 x 0.7 cms. Manganese.

522. Bristol.** 1720-50.
13 x 0.9 cms. Manganese. Similar to (Ray, no. 50).

ELIJAH CARRIED UP TO HEAVEN: 2 Kings 2 v. 12

523. London.* 1720-50.
12.5 x 0.8 cms. Shiny Blue.

524. Bristol.** 1720-50.
13 x 0.7 cms. Blue. (cf. Ray, no. 51).

London/Liverpool

THE MOCKING OF ELISHA: 2 Kings 2 v. 23

525. London.** 1720-50.
12.8 x 0.9 cms. Blue. Elisha was mocked for being bald, but in this instance the artist has given him a full head of hair. Similar fragments have been found in Lambeth (cf. Ray, fig. 22 p. 98).

526. Liverpool.** 1745-60.
12.5 x 0.8 cms. (Cut down). Manganese. cf. Ray, no. 54.

527. Liverpool.** 1750-70.
12.7 x 0.7 cms. Blue.

528. Liverpool.** 1750-70.
12.7 x 0.7cms. Blue. Very similar but with only one child. (cf. Ray, no. 53).

THE DEATH OF JEZEBEL: 2 Kings 9 v. 36

529. London.** 1740-60.
12.8 x 0.7 cms. Blue. cf. Ray, no. 52.

A CORPSE, THROWN INTO ELISHA'S GRAVE, REVIVES: 2 Kings 13 v. 21

530. London.** 1760-80.
12.5 x 0.7 cms. Blue. (cf. Ray, no. 55).

531. Liverpool.** 1770-90.
12.6 x 0.7 cms. Blue.

ESTHER BEFORE AHASUERUS: Esther 5 v. 2

532. London.* Late 17th century. 12.6 x 0.9 cms. Blue. Similar corners have been found in London (Ray, p. 99 fig. 25). Compare with tile no. **14** & **536**.

533. London.* Late 17th century. 12.6 x 0.9 cms. Blue. Similar to **532** but without the figure. cf. no. **15**.

534. Bristol.** 1720-50. 13.2 x 0.8 cms. Blue.

THE TRIALS OF JOB: Job 1

535. London.** 1740-60. Manganese.

JOB SMITTEN WITH BOILS: Job 2 v. 7

536. London.* Late 17th century. 12.6 x 0.9 cms. Bright Blue. This is part of the same set as no. **14** and no. **532**. For a later London version (cf. Ray, no. 57).

537. Liverpool.* 1750-70. Blue.

THE AVENGING ANGEL: Ezekiel 39 v. 3

538. Liverpool.** 1750-70. Bright Blue, Blue corners. Powdered Manganese Border.

London/Liverpool

JONAH AND THE WHALE: Jonah 2 v. 10

539. London.* 1730-50.
12.7 x 0.7 cms. Blue.

JONAH UNDER THE GOURD: Jonah 4 v. 6

540. London.* 1700-20.
12 x 0.8 cms. Shiny Bright Blue. The colour of the body and size is comparable with nos. **74, 506** and **622,** although the painting is different. The glaze is uneven and pitted.

541. London.* 1720-50.
12.9 x 0.8 cms. Shiny Blue.

542. London.** 1750-70.
12.5 x 0.7 cms. Blue.

543. Liverpool.** 1750-70.
12.5 x 0.8 cms. Blue. (cf. Ray, no. 61) for a different Liverpool version with a studded border.

DANIEL IN THE LION'S DEN: Daniel 6 v. 16

544. London.** 1740-60.
Blue. Similar to Ray, no. 59.

545. Liverpool.** 1750-70.
12.5 x 0.8 cms. Blue. cf. no. **555** and **517.**

TOBIAS CATCHING THE FISH: Tobias 6 v. 3

546. London.* 1740-60.
12.5 x 0.8 cms. Blue.

547. London.** 1740-60.
12.4 x 0.8 cms. Shiny Blue. Fragments of this subject but with a different border have been found in Lambeth (cf. Ray fig. 23). For a similar tile (cf. Ray no. 62).

TOBIAS AND THE ANGEL RAPHAEL: Tobias 6

548. Liverpool.** 1750-70.
12.7 x 0.6 cms. Blue. This is probably the same subject as the previous tiles but the artist has omitted the fish.

TOBIAS AND THE ANGEL BURNING THE FISH'S GALL: Tobias 6 v. 5

551. Probably English London.* 1700-30.
12.9 x 0.7 cms. Blue. Unusual corners.

TOBIAS AND THE ANGEL: Tobias 11 v. 4

549. London.* 1700-30.
12.6 x 0.9 cms. Blue. A substantial tile with a slightly pinky glaze. The back is rough but there are no pinholes.

550. London.** 1750-70.
12.7 x 0.7 cms. Blue. For same subject but without a border, (cf. Ray, no. 63).

London/Bristol/Liverpool

JUDITH WITH THE HEAD OF HOLOFERNES: Judith 13 v. 10

552. London.* 1700-30.
12.5 x 1.0 cms. Blue. (cf. Ray, no. 64).

553. London.** 1730-50.
13 x 0.8 cms. Manganese. Note Judith is holding a sword.

554. Bristol.** 1720-50.
13.01 x 0.9 cms. Blue.

555. Liverpool.** 1750-70.
12.9 x 0.7 cms. Blue. cf. no. **545.**

SUSANNA AND THE ELDERS:
Apocrypha "The History of Susanna" v. 15-16

556. London.** 1750-70.
12.7 x 0.8 cms. Blue.

DANIEL SUMMONED HIS SERVANTS TO STREW ASHES THROUGH THE TEMPLE: Apocrypha "Bel and the Dragon" v. 14

557. London.** 1700-20.
12.8 x 0.8 cms. Blue.

UNIDENTIFIED SUBJECT

558. London. 1700-20.
12.8 x 0.9 cms. Blue.

NEW TESTAMENT

THE ANNUNCIATION: Luke 1 v. 28

559. London.** 1700-20.
12 x 0.9 cms. Blue. This is a small tile, cf. no. **540**.

560. London.* Early 18th century.
12.3 x 0.8 cms. Unusual Pale Blue and the painting is different.

561. London.** 1720-50.
12.9 x 0.8 cms. Shiny Blue. This is the more common form. (cf. Ray, no. 66).

THE THREE KINGS FOLLOW THE STAR: Matthew 2 v. 9

Fig. XVII. A delftware tea caddy decorated in blue with a scene of The Three King's, cf. no. **562**. Height 8.8 x 6.2 x 8.3 cms., circa 1710. London.** (See fig. XV p. 80 for the reverse side). It is unusual to find the exact tile subject reproduced on hollow ware.

562. London.** 1720-50.
12.8 x 0.8 cms. Blue.

THE ADORATION OF THE SHEPHERDS: Luke 2 v. 16

563. London.** 1720-50.
12.8 x 0.8 cms. Blue. For a slightly later version, (cf. Ray, no. 64).

THE FLIGHT INTO EYGPT: Matthew 2 v. 9

564. London.* 1720-50.
12.9 x 0.7 cms. Manganese.

London/Bristol/Liverpool

THE CIRCUMCISION: Luke 2 v. 21

565. London.** 1740-60.
12.5 x 0.7 cms. Blue.

566. Bristol.** 1720-30.
13 x 0.7 cms. Blue. For another Bristol version of this subject, (cf. Ray, no. 68).

THE PRESENTATION OF CHRIST IN THE TEMPLE: Luke 2 v. 22

567. London.** 1750-70.
12.4 x 0.6 cms. Blue.

THE BAPTISM OF CHRIST: Matthew 3 v. 16

568. London.** 1740-60.
12.5 x 0.8 cms. Manganese. (cf. Ray, no. 70).

569. Bristol.** 1720-50.
13 x 0.8 cms. Blue.

570. Liverpool.** 1760-80.
12.7 x 0.6 cms. Blue.

THE TEMPTATION IN THE WILDERNESS: Matthew 4 v. 3

571. London.** 1740-60.
12.8 x 0.8 cms. Blue. (Ray no. 71) for a Bristol version in reverse.

572. Liverpool.** 1740-60.
12.7 x 0.8 cms. Manganese. cf. no. **526**.

THE FISHERMEN LET DOWN THEIR NET: Luke 5 v. 5

573. Liverpool.** 1750-70.
12.8 x 0.8 cms. Blue. For the same subject with an octagonal dash border (cf. Horne no. 77), cf. no. **623**.

THE WASHING OF CHRIST'S FEET: Luke 7 v. 36

574. Bristol.** 1730-50.
13 x 0.9 cms. Blue.

THE GADARENE SWINE: Luke 8 v. 33

575. Liverpool.** 1760-80.
12.5 x 0.7 cms. Blue.

THE GOOD SAMARITAN: Luke 10 v. 33

576. London.* 1740-60.
Dark Blue. For a Liverpool version see (Ray, no. 79).

577. Liverpool. 1750-70.
12.7 x 0.7 cms. approx. Blue. Very like a Dutch tile though the glaze looks English. A large '3P' is painted in black on the reverse.

London/Bristol/Liverpool

CHRIST DRIVING OUT THE DEVIL: Luke 9 v. 42

578. London.** 1740-60.
12.6 x 0.8 cms. Blue. The demon can be seen coming out the child's head. (cf. Ray, no. 73).

THE WOMAN HEALED OF AN ISSUE OF BLOOD: Matthew 9 v. 22

579. Bristol.** 1730-50.
12.8 x 0.8 cms. Blue. For the same subject on a London tile (cf. Ray, no. 74).

580. Liverpool.** 1750-70.
12.8 x 0.7 cms. Blue.

THE PARABLE OF THE SOWER: Matthew 14 v. 24

581. London.** 1750-70.
12.6 x 0.7cms. Blue (cf. Ray, no. 72).

CHRIST AND THE WOMEN OF CANAAN: Matthew 15 v. 21-28

582. London.* 1740-60.
12.6 x 0.8 cms. Blue. The reason for the "32" on the post is unknown.

583. London.** 1730-50.
12.7 x 0.8 cms. Manganese.

London/Liverpool

SALOME WITH THE HEAD OF JOHN THE BAPTIST: Mark 6 v. 28

584. London.** 1730-50.
12.8 x 0.8 cms. Blue. (Courtesy of Liverpool Museum).

THE MIRACLE OF THE LOAVES AND FISHES: John 6 v. 1-13

585. London.* 1720-50.
12.9 x 0.9 cms. Blue. Note the multitude standing in the background.

586. London.* 1740-60.
12.9 x 0.6 cms. Manganese. The 'fishes' are clearly painted.

587. Liverpool.** 1750-70.
12.6 x 0.7 cms. Blue. (cf. Ray, no. 77).

PETER WALKING ON WATER: Matthew 14 v. 30

588. Liverpool.** 1760-80.
12.5 x 0.7 cms. Blue. For a Bristol version (cf. Ray, no. 78).

PETER WITH THE KEYS TO THE KINGDOM ON EARTH: Matthew 16 v. 18-19

589. Liverpool.** 1750-80.
12.7 x 0.7 cms. Blue.

Liverpool/London

PETER TAKING MONEY OUT OF THE FISH'S MOUTH:
Mathew 17 v. 27

MATTHEW

590. Liverpool.** 1750-70.
12.9 x 0.6 cms. Dark Blue.

591. Liverpool.** 1750-70.
12.7 x 0.7 cms. Blue.

"BRING IN THE POOR FROM THE HIGHWAYS": Luke 14 v. 23

592. Liverpool.** 1750-80.
12.7 x 0.6 cms. Blue. (Courtesy of Hants Museum Service Ref. no. DA 1979. 75/64).

THE LOST SHEEP: Luke 15 v. 5

593. Liverpool.** 1760-70.
12.7 x 0.7 cms. Blue. Also found on Dutch tiles. (cf. Ray no. 80).

THE PRODIGAL SON IN MISERY: Luke 15 v. 15-16

594. London.** 1740-60.
12.5 x 0.7 cms. Blue.

THE RETURN OF THE PRODIGAL SON: Luke 15 v. 20

595. London.* 1720-50.
12.9 x 0.9 cms. Blue. Similar to (Ray, no. 84).

596. Liverpool.** 1750-70.
12.5 x 0.7 cms. Blue.

DIVES AND LAZARUS: Luke 16 v. 20

597. Bristol.** 1740-60.
13.1 x 0.7 cms. Blue.

LAZARUS IN HEAVEN, DIVES IN HELL: Luke 16 v. 22

  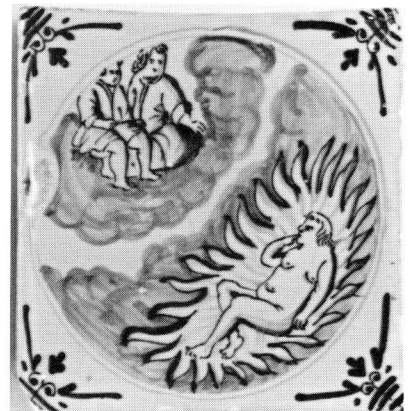

598. London.* Possibly circa 1680.
12.6 x 0.9 cms. Light Blue. cf. no. **474**.

599. London.* 1720-50.
12.7 x 0.8 cms. Blue.

600. London.* 1730-50.
12.9 x 0.9 cms. Manganese.

601. London.** 1730-50.
12.6 x 0.9 cms. Blue. Powdered Mang.

602. Bristol.** 1750-70.
12 x 0.8 cms. Blue. cf. no. **597**.

603. Liverpool.* 1750-70.
12.6 x 0.9 cms. Blue. Only the rich man.

London/Liverpool/Bristol

THE DUTIFUL SERVANT:
Luke 17 v. 7-10

604. London.** 1740-60.
12.7 x 0.7 cms. Blue.

JESUS AND THE LEPER:
Mark 1 v. 40-41.

605. Liverpool.** 1750-70.
13 x 0.6 cms. Manganese.

ZACCHAEUS UP A TREE: Luke 19 v. 5

606. London.** 1750-70.
12.9 x 0.7 cms. Blue. (Courtesy of Liverpool Museum).

CHRIST HEALING THE BLIND MAN: John 9 v. 5

607. London.** 1740-60.
12.8 x 0.7 cms. Blue.

608. Bristol.** 1740-70.
13.2 x 0.8 cms. Blue.

609. Liverpool.** 1750-70.
12.6 x 0.6 cms. Blue.

610. London.* 1740-60.
12.8 x 0.8 cms. Manganese. These are probably another interpretation of the same scene.

611. London.* 1750-70.
12.4 x 0.6 cms. Blue.

London/Liverpool/Bristol

JESUS AND THE WOMAN OF SAMARIA: John 4 v. 5

612. London.** 1740-60.
12.3 x 0.8 cms. Blue. (cf. Britton, no. 215).

613. Liverpool.** 1740-60.
12.8 x 0.8 cms. Manganese. The mark 'C' in blue on the reverse.

614. Liverpool.** 1750-70.
12.7 x 0.8 cms. Blue.

THE CLEANSING OF THE TEMPLE: Matthew 21 v. 12

615. London.* 1740-60.
12.9 x 0.9 cms. Blue.

616. Bristol.** 1720-50.
13 x 0.7 cms. Blue. For a similar London tile (cf. Ray no. 86).

CHRIST AND THE TRIBUTE MONEY: Mark 12 v. 13-17

617. London.** 1750-70.
12.9 x 0.6 cms. Manganese.

THE WISE VIRGINS: Matthew 25 v. 1-13

618. Bristol.** 1730-50.
12.4 x 0.7 cms. Blue.

London/Liverpool

CHRIST WASHING THE DISCIPLES' FEET: John 13 v. 5

619. London.** 1740-60.
12.8 x 0.8 cms. Blue.

620. London.** 1740-60.
12.6 x 0.7 cms. Blue. (cf. Ray, no. 88) for a different Bristol design.

CHRIST IN THE GARDEN OF GETHSEMANE: Mark 14 v. 35

621. Liverpool.** 1750-70.
12.8 x 0.8 cms. Blue.

ST. PETER'S DENIAL OF CHRIST: Matthew 26 v. 73

622. London.** 1720-50.
12.1 x 0.8 cms. Blue. This is a small tile. Compare with nos. **74, 506** and **540**. For a slightly later version (cf. Horne, no. 82).

623. Liverpool.** 1750-70.
12.9 x 0.6 cms. Blue. Compare with no. **573.**

JUDAS HANGS HIMSELF: Matthew 27 v. 5

624. London.* 1750-70.
12.7 x 0.8 cms. Blue.

English?/London/Bristol/Liverpool

PONTIUS PILATE WASHING HIS HANDS: Matthew 27 v. 29

625. Possibly English/London. Circa 1680.
12.6 x 0.8 cms. Blue with pinky glaze.

626. London.* 1700-30.
12.8 x 0.9 cms. Blue. (cf. Ray, no. 89).

627. Bristol.** 1730-50.
13.2 x 0.8 cms. Blue.

CHRIST AT THE COLUMN: John 19 v. 1

628. London.** 1720-50.
12.9 x 0.9 cms. Blue. For a Bristol version with the subject in reverse (cf. Ray no. 90).

CHRIST CARRYING THE CROSS: John 19 v. 17

629. London.* Late 17th century.
12.5 x 0.7 cms. Blue. Same set as no. **15**.

630. London.* 1720-50.
13 x 0.9 cms. Blue.

631. Bristol.** 1720-50.
12.8 x 0.8 cms. Blue. (cf. Ray, no. 91).

632. Bristol.** 1740-60.
13 x 0.8 cms. Blue.

633. Liverpool.** 1750-70.
12.9 x 0.7 cms. Blue.

634. Liverpool.** 1760-80.
12.9 x 0.7 cms. Blue.

London/Bristol/Liverpool

THE CRUCIFIXION: John 19 v. 26

635. London. ** 1720-50.
12.6 x 0.8 cms. Blue. "INRI" at the head of the cross signifies Jesus of Nazareth, King of the Jews, from the Latin. A fragment of a plate dated 1701 with a similar decoration was found by Garner in Lambeth (Lipski, no. 230).

636. Bristol. ** 1740-60.
13 x 0.8 cms. Blue. Similar to no. **635** but reversed, also inscribed "INRI."

637. London. ** 1740-60.
12.8 x 0.8cms. Manganese. "IHS" at the head of the Cross are the first three capital letters in Greek for the name Jesus.

638. Liverpool. ** 1750-70.
12.6 x 0.7 cms. Blue. For a Liverpool tile without a border, (cf. Ray, no. 92).

639. Liverpool. ** 1740-70.
Blue. An unusual version.

640. Liverpool. ** 1740-60.
12.8 x 0.9 cms. Manganese with red blood issuing from Christ's hands, feet and wound. This is most unusual and more commonly found on Dutch Delft. The background is typical of a Liverpool scene. cf. no. **652**.

The Crucifixion is one of the few subjects that also appears on delftware plates. Lipski lists five dated plates ranging from 1698 until 1749 (Lipski, nos. 215, 230, 513, 527 and 528), all of which are similar to the illustrated tiles. (A slightly different interpretation is shown on a tile in Britton, no. 219).

THE ENTOMBMENT: John 19 v. 41

641. London. ** 1740-60.
12.6 x 0.8 cms. Blue. (cf. Ray, no. 93).

106

CHRIST APPEARING TO MARY MAGDALENE: John 20 v. 15

642. London.* 1720-50.
12.7 x 0.9 cms. Blue. (Ray, no. 95 and fig. 38) illustrates tiles painted with a similar scene.

643. Bristol.** 1740-60.
13 x 0.8 cms. Manganese.

644. Liverpool.** 1750-70.
12.5 x 0.6 cms. Blue.

CHRIST ON THE ROAD TO EMMAUS: Mark 16 v. 12

645. London.** 1750-70.
12.5 x 0.7 cms. Blue.

Fig. XVIII. A tinglazed plate decorated in blue illustrating the Ascension of Christ into Heaven. Diameter 21.8 cms. Circa 1750. Liverpool. The rather pale blue with a dark red enamelled rim is typical of Liverpool.

THE ASCENSION: Luke 24 v. 51

646. London.* Early 18th century.
12.9 x 0.7 cms. Blue on white ground. This has an unusual corner and is painted on a reddish body.

647. London.** 1740-70.
12.8 x 0.6 cms. Blue.

648. Bristol.** 1740-60.
13 x 0.9 cms. Blue.

London/Bristol/Liverpool

PETER AND JOHN HEAL A CRIPPLE AT THE GATE OF THE TEMPLE: Acts 3 v. 1-8

649. London.* 1750-70.
12.7 x 0.7 cms. Blue.

THE STONING OF STEPHEN: Acts 7 v. 59

650. London.* 1730-50.
12.7 x 0.8 cms. Blue. (Courtesy of Hants Museum Service Ref. DA. 1985. 98/2).

651. Bristol.** 1740-60.
13.2 x 0.7 cms. Blue. (Ray, no. 97).

652. Liverpool.** 1740-70.
12.5 x 0.8 cms. Manganese. Part of the same set as no. **639**.

ST. PHILIP BAPTISING THE EUNUCH: Acts 8 v. 38

653. London.** 1700-30.
12.7 x 0.8 cms. Blue.

ST. PAUL ESCAPING FROM DAMASCUS: Acts 9 v. 24.

654. London.* 1740-60.
12.2 x 0.8 cms. Manganese. (cf. Ray no. 98).

655. London.** 1740-60.
12.8 x 0.7 cms. Manganese.

656. London. 1740-60.
13.1 x 0.9 cms. Manganese.

ST. PETER'S VISION AT JOPPA: Acts 11 v. 5-10

657. London.** 1740-60.
12.5 x 0.8 cms. Blue.

AN ANGEL APPEARS TO RELEASE ST. PETER FROM PRISON: Acts 12 v. 7

658. London.* 1700-30.
12.8 x 0.8 cms. Blue.

659. Bristol.** 1740-60.
approx. 12.9 x 0.8 cms. (cut down). Blue.

ST. PETER ESCAPES FROM PRISON. Acts 12 v. 10

660. London.* 1700-20.
13.2 x 0.9 cms. Blue. (Ray, fig. 30b)
illustrates a fragment found in Bristol
painted with this subject. Also similar to
(Ray no. 99).

661. Liverpool.** 1750-80.
12.8 x 0.6 cms. Blue. Large number '3'
painted in black on the reverse.

UNIDENTIFIED ANGEL

662. Liverpool.** 1750-70.
12.8 x 0.7 cms. Blue. 'N' in black on
reverse.

ST. PAUL BEING BITTEN BY A VIPER: Acts 28 v. 2-3

663. London.* 1740-60.
12.7 x 0.7 cms. Blue.

Bristol/London

RECESS TILES

It has long been a point of discussion as to what these "recessed tiles" were used for. They seem to have little practical use being too shallow to a take a candle or soap and were therefore probably intended as decoration; to make a focal point within a tiled niche or to break up an otherwise flat row of tiles.

It was fashionable during the mid 18th century to have a **tiled wash-basin alcove** and several of these have survived. An example formerly in the Lipski Collection and now in the Victoria and Albert Museum, also includes four recess tiles, and another example illustrated in Ray (page 32) includes a recess tile. The Ashmolean Museum ("Warren Collection" Ray, Pl. 92) has an alcove of 49 tiles, 7 x 7, whilst another can be seen in a house in Bath (north east corner of Queen's Square), this alcove is 10 tiles across by 8 high, decorated in blue with a Louis XV border and cross hatched corners (cf. p. 45).

The size and thickness of these recess tiles varies considerably and the difference in painting styles suggests that they were made over a period of twenty or thirty years. The overall size of each recess tile was made to take up the space of two ordinary tiles and in certain instances the border decoration as in no. **673** was painted to match in with the surrounding tiles.

Tile no. **664** is in a class of its own and is the only example known that has been made without a base (edge glazed over). The colour of the glaze, style of painting and corner motif tie in with tile no. **343** which has been attributed to Bristol.

No. **665** is painted with the scene of a lady seated in an early 18th century chair and drinking from a baluster stemmed glass. Unfortunately the corner motif and edging pattern does not tie up with any other known tiles although the figure has been copied from the same source as no. **666** (probably an engraving).

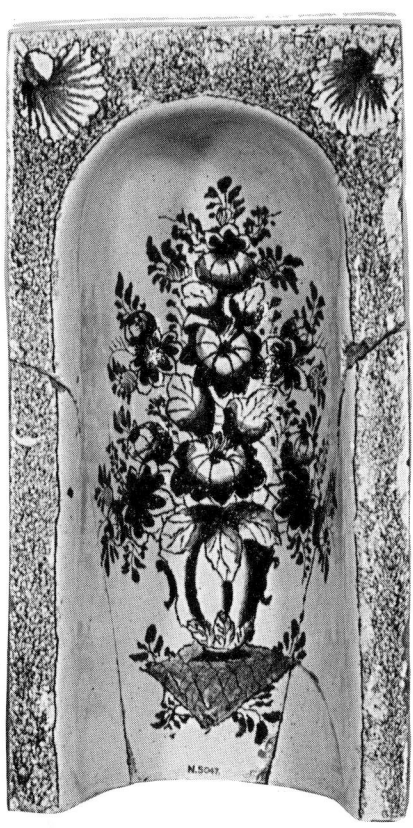

664. Bristol.** 1730-50.
24.6 x 12.6 x 0.7 cms. Depth: 6.6 cms.
Dark Blue powdered Manganese, glazed on back. (Bristol N5047).
This is the only example that has no base (the edge being glazed over). The painting style, colour and corner motif tie in with tile no. **343**, page 63. (Reproduced by kind permission of Bristol Museum & Art Gallery).

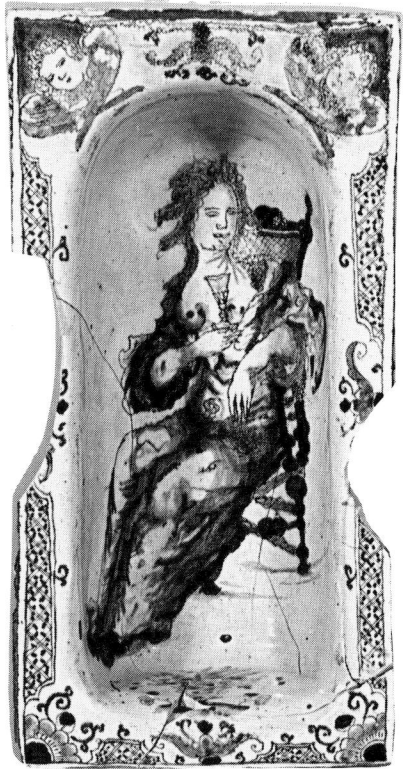

665. London or Bristol. 1730-50.
24.3 x 12.2 x 0.6 cms. Depth: 6.0 cms.
Blue, not glazed on back. (Bristol Q1965).
The lady here is shown seated in an early 18th century chair, drinking from a baluster stemmed glass. This tile was originally in a tiled niche which came out of a Bristol house (Ray, p. 32) but as other tiles from this set were Liverpool, larger and probably later, it seems likely that this was not its original setting. (Reproduced by kind permission of Bristol Museum & Art Gallery).

666. London.* 1735-45.
25.5 cms. high. Blue, powdered Manganese surround. One of a pair sold at Christie's June 1986. The lady is similar to no. **665.** The segmented trellis and scroll pattern over her head was also used on manganese and blue plates (see fig. III, page 24). For a similar plate dated 1741 see (Lipski, no. 475). (Reproduced by kind permission of Christie's).

667. London or Bristol. 1735-45.
25.4 x 12.2 approx. Blue with powdered Manganese surround. (Reproduced by kind permission of Hy Duke & Son, Dorchester).

The painting of no. **666** is less detailed, but the inclusion of the segmented trellis and scroll pattern in association with the powdered manganese can be compared with certain delftware plates (Fig. III, p. 24) and a similar plate dated 1741 (Lipski 475) (The Segmented Trellis and Scroll pattern was also used on tiles, cf. no. **425**).

The classical figure painted on no. **667** is of the same type as four recess tiles which form part of the Lipski tile niche in the Victoria & Albert Museum. These are all painted with different draped classical figures but all have the same segmented fan with a grotesque face.

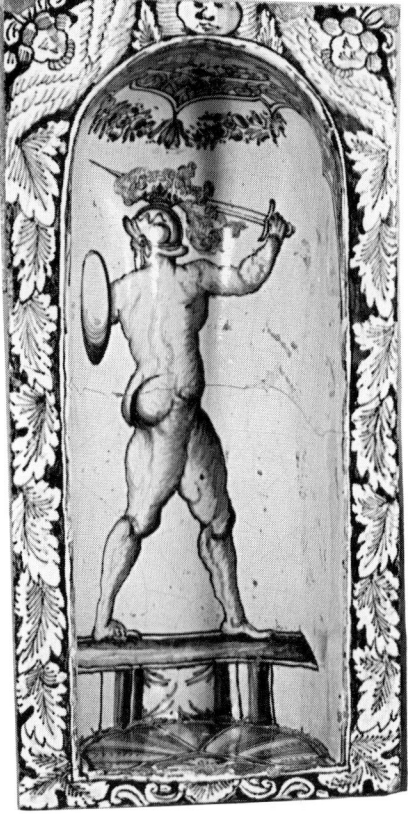  

668. London or Bristol. 1735-45. 25.8 x 12.9 x 0.6 cms. Depth: 7.9 cms. Dark Blue, not glazed on back. (Bristol N5691).

669. London or Bristol. 1735-45. 25.8 x 12.9 x 0.6 cms. Dark Blue. Not glazed on back. (Bristol N5692).

670. London or Bristol. 1735-45. 25.8 x 13 cms. Depth: 7.8 cms. Blue, not glazed on back (DA 1980-60). Very similar to nos. **668** and **669** and also about the same size; this had at one time been one of a pair. (Reproduced by kind permission of Hants County Museum Service).

Both nos. **668** and **669** were removed from the same house, 3 Unity St. Bristol, and are very similar in style. One has a segmented fan design at the top of the recess and the other has a little chinoiserie scene. The shell motif at the base emphasizes the depth of the niche. The figure on no. **669** also appears on no. **670**. (Reproduced by kind permission of Bristol Museum & Art Gallery).

The figure on no. **669** also appears on recess tile no. **670** from the Hampshire County Museum Service Collection at Alton. In this instance the border is painted to look like a stone niche and has the grotesque face above the figure with lengths of "fabric" forming a fan. Tile, no. **668** with its partner, no. **669**, are both painted with classical figures which were rarely used on English delftware although parallels could perhaps be drawn with the figures included on the Saffron Walden tile panels dated 1739 (Lipski, nos. 1695-1696), and the delftware tray illustrated in ("Fair as China Dishes", no. 62) and now in the Victoria & Albert Museum. (Two classical statues standing on square bases are included in a large 66 tile picture which was probably painted around 1720-30 (Victoria & Albert Museum, see notes on p. 117) and one of these figures is similar to the Venus on tiles **671** and **672** although there is probably a difference in date of some thirty years.

671. Bristol.* 1750-70.
25.5 x 12.7 x 0.9 cms. Depth: 6.2 cms. Blue, partly glazed on back. Two similar recess tiles but with different borders can be seen at the Red Lodge, Bristol.

672. Liverpool.* 1750-70.
25.5 x 12.3 x 0.6 cms. Depth: 5.8 cms. Blue, glazed on the back. One of a pair (Bristol G116). Compare the borders on page 42. (Reproduced by kind permission of Bristol Museum & Art Gallery).

673. Liverpool or Bristol. 1760-70.
26.2 x 13.2 x 1.0 cms. Depth: 7.0 cms. Blue, not glazed on back. (Bristol N5693) The **Studded border** is painted so that the pattern will continue on to the next tile. cf. nos. **183-184**. The rather white glaze suggests Liverpool although the size of 13.20 cms. is the same as the large tiles being produced in Bristol. The border was made in Bristol and Liverpool. (Reproduced by kind permission of Bristol Museum & Art Gallery).

The subject of Venus and Cupid was popular on recess tiles and was certainly made in Bristol; a polychrome example having been seen in a private collection which shows the figures painted in manganese and blue and the flange decorated with flowers in typical Bristol "Fazackerly type" colours (length 26.6 x 13 x 0.8 cms.). The painting is similar to that on no. **671** although the 'pineapple' corner motif on this example cannot be exactly parallelled (cf. nos. **417** and **418**). There are two more similar recess tiles in the Red Lodge, Bristol, these having borders of elaborate scrolls and leaves. The same Venus scene was used on the recess tile in the Ashmolean Museum ("English Delftware Pottery", Ray, no. 191) although the size of this, 26 x 13.4 cms. is considerably larger than another similar one recorded in a private collection that was only 24.9 x 12.4 cms. The Venus figure on no. **672** has been painted in reverse and is standing on a slightly more elaborate plinth. This variation should be considered and also the use of the dash border which is more usually associated with Liverpool tiles (see p. 42). The white glaze of no. **673** is more typically Liverpool although the studded border may also have been used at Bristol.

In conclusion it must be said that to categorize these recess tiles is very difficult although it does seem likely that they were made over a period of some 30 odd years and that they were not all made in Bristol as had previously been assumed.

London

674. A panel of 66 tiles (each approximately 12.6 cms. sq.) depicting a vase of flowers 1720-30 London.** The reverse side of every tile being clearly numbered for easy assembly.

Another panel of 66 tiles and by the same painter is in the Museum of London collection (cf. Britton, p. 180). This example includes the same exotic birds and also has an area of elaborate leaf design painted on a dark blue ground which is similar to a design found on a tankard dated 1728 (Lipski, no. 814). Another tankard, dated 1727 (Lipski, no. 810) is painted with the same type of flowers to that found on these panels, a pattern often used on straight sided delftware bowls of the early 18th century. A similar panel of 44 tiles is in the Victoria and Albert Museum, see notes on page 117. The vase of flower design appears repeatedly on individual tiles (pp. 60-63).

675. A panel of 66 tiles showing a European landscape scene. Each tile approximately 12.5 cms. sq. 1720-30 London.** The reverse side of every tile is clearly numbered for easy assembly.

This panel compares with another tile picture in the Museum of London (see Britton, p. 181) and a similar one of the same size in the Victoria & Albert Museum. All these pictures and including no. **674** are of a very similar type and obviously come from the same workshop. A fragment of a tile showing a European figure leaning against a fence was found at Vauxhall by Denis Cockell and may have come from a similar tile panel (E.C.C. Vol. 9 Part 2, 1974, Pl. 135). (See notes on page 117).

TILE PICTURES

It was fashionable in Holland during the 17th century to decorate entire walls with tiles. Some Dutch tile pictures consist of over 400 tiles, and apart from being attractive they served a purpose in helping to disguise the damp which was a real problem caused through building on low lying land. In England production was undertaken on a much smaller scale, and the largest recorded panel contained 96 tiles ("Griffith 1751", see p. 119).
The manufacture of tiles is a skilled art and during the late 17th and early 18th century the English potters were having undoubted difficulties in production, therefore it seems likely that the earliest tile pictures were undertaken by craftsmen imported from the Continent (see p. 5).

London

It must have been an everyday sight during the 18th century to see permanent advertisements painted on tiles that could be kept fresh and clean. The "Dish of Coffee Boy" pictured (front cover) is one of these rare survivors and probably dates from the early 18th century. Only eight tiles remain from the original picture, which if the border design is followed, must have consisted of at least 24 tiles. On the table which is covered by a cloth rest a number of interesting items which at one time included a candlestick (now missing) but whose light rays are just visible on the left hand edge; a newspaper on which can be seen the letters "-AZET", possibly the London Gazette; a mug that may be delftware; a glass wine bottle which can be dated to around 1700; a small bowl or dish of coffee that might be Chinese or delftware and two clay pipes. The boy is wearing a high heeled shoe very similar to those copied in delftware (for an example dated 1710, see "Britton" no. 114). Edward Robinson's "Early History of Coffee Houses in England 1893", says of it on plate 236: "Mr. James Smith, an old collector, well remembers it was formerly in Baxter's Coffee Rooms, no. 66 Brick Lane, Spitalfields. The house in question was ancient and possessed a single bay window. The tiling was let into the right hand wall at a height of about five feet from the ground, and was opposite to the wooden seats provided for customers just inside the front room". Bryant Lillywhite's "London Coffee Houses" says that the picture came from Baxter's, "but must have come from one of the earlier coffee houses". Baxter's flourished in the nineteenth century. Another tile panel in the Museum of London Collection and dating from this early period is an inn sign made for the Cock and Bottle which is reputed to have stood in Cannon Street (Britton, no. 203). This picture consists of 24 tiles, 6 x 4 with half size border tiles and quarter tiles for the corners.

It is known that Nathaniel Oade of the Gravel Lane Pottery, Southwark, brought a Dutchman to England in circa 1718 in order to make tiles (see p. 5) and it is also known from Oade's inventory ("Britton", Appendix III p. 190) that he was producing a large number of tiles in 1726. (Also in this document is mentioned the "Tyld Parlour" which one can presume was decorated with tiles made on the premises). The Gravel Lane pottery had the skill and therefore must be considered as a candidate for the manufacture of some or all of the next group of tile pictures to be discussed.

In 1912 six tile panels were recovered from the pantry of the demolished dwelling house attached to Daun and Vallentin's Lambeth Distillery in Church Street, opposite Lambeth Parish Church and adjacent to the Norfolk House pottery. It appears that these panels were set up in about 1800 and although the owner had always understood that they had come from Strawberry Hill House, there is no evidence to support this, either from Horace Walpole's detailed description or from the house sale catalogues. Three of these tile panels were purchased by the Victoria and Albert Museum and consist of:

1) A panel of 44 tiles, Vase of Flowers (V & A ref. no. C196. 1912).
2) A panel of 66 tiles, European Figures in a Landscape (V & A ref. no. C195. 1912).
3) A panel of 55 tiles, Chinoiserie stylized River Scene (V & A ref. no. C194. 1912). (Illustrated in "Tiles", Lane, Pl. 37B) pair to no. **676.**

Two more of these panels are now in the Museum of London.

4) A panel of 66 tiles, Vase of Flowers (M of L ref. no. 10359) (Britton, no. 205).
5) A panel of 66 tiles, European Figures in a Landscape (M of L ref. no. 10358) (Britton, no. 206).

The sixth panel hung for many years at Doulton House, Lambeth and is illustrated here on page 118. This 55 tile panel shows a stylized oriental river scene and is the pair to the panel in the Victoria and Albert Museum mentioned above (ref. C194. 1912).

Two more panels have recently been discovered, both consisting of 66 tiles. The Vase of Flowers panel on page 114 came out of a country saleroom but the recovery of the European Landscape Panel on page 115 is quite remarkable. Tiles from this picture have been gathered together for over ten years from as many different sources including, Sotheby's, Christie's, Phillips, the Lipski Collection, other private collectors, country sales, Portobello Road etc., and the picture is now complete but for three tiles. This fine panel has incidentally been painted by a left handed artist and is very similar to the landscape panel at the Museum of London (MOL 10358).

Eight virtually complete tile pictures of this type have now been recorded and they are all quite clearly related, the tiles being all very similar with two pinholes on the front and painted in a distinctive dark blue with a glossy surface. The shape and composition of the painted scenes suggests that they were probably all made in pairs, and were intended to be hung accordingly.

Tile pictures continued to be made in London certainly well into the second half of the 18th century although very few examples have survived. A pair of blue tile pictures, each 5 tiles x 8 (Saffron Walden Museum) once adorned the local "Old Swan Inn". One of these panels was painted to commemorate the birth of Prince Edward, Duke of York in 1739 and is signed 'WE' 1739 and the companion panel commemorates the stay of Oliver Cromwell in Saffron Walden in 1645 (Lipski, no. 1695/6).

It is known that William Griffith's factory at Lambeth High Street was making tile pictures during the mid 18th century as a large panel consisting of 96 tiles and inscribed 'Griffith 1751' once adorned an arched niche above the main door (Britton, colour Pl. T). The inscribed panel, no. **677,** also served the same purpose albeit on a more modest scale. The original tiles that remain of this panel are clearly numbered on the back and it has been possible to interpret the original inscription by comparing the wording used on bill heads of the day, (see fig. XX). The two tiles, no. **678,** show a horseman outside a tavern, "The Sign of the Horseshoe". This is part of something much bigger and must date to the last quarter of the 18th century. The rural scene painted in dark blue is typical of wares being produced in Lambeth at this time (cf. Lipski, no. 858 a mug dated 1785 and no. 860 a mug dated 1786).

London

676. A panel consisting of 55 tiles painted with a stylized oriental river scene, each tile being numbered on the reverse and approximately 12.6 cms. sq. circa 1720-30 London.**
The Victoria & Albert Museum has the pair to this panel which they bought in 1912 and is illustrated in "Tiles"—Lane, page 137B. See notes on page 117.

677. Part of a trade sign painted on tinglazed tiles. London.** 1740-60. Each tile is approximately 12.4 cms. sq. and has a number on the reverse (fig. XIX). The missing letters have been construed from a typical trade card of the day, (fig. XX).

Two tiles from a similar panel are in the Saffron Walden Museum. One has the letters 'OF' with the number 8 on the reverse, and the second has 'SS&' with the number 18 on the reverse.

Fig. XIX. The reverse side of the trade sign no. **677** is clearly marked with large numbers which helped when reconstructing the inscription.

	3	4	5		
	8	9		11	12
		16			

Fig. XX. A typical trade card as used during the mid 18th century.

London/Bristol

678. Two tiles from a larger picture painted in strong blue. 12.9 x 0.7 cms. 1770-90. London.** Compare with a mug dated 1785 (Lipski no. 858). See notes on page 117.

Bristol

The Victoria and Albert Museum has a very fine tile picture painted with a view of the church of St. Mary Redcliff, at Bristol, originally 6 tiles long by 4 high ("Tiles"—Lane, Pl. 36 and "English Delftware Pottery"—Ray, fig. 11). The layout of the scene suggests that it was copied from a print. Who commissioned it is unknown, although the picture does include the arms of Bishop Butler (1738-1753) which gives a guide for dating. It was retrieved with difficulty from the window sill of a butcher's shop in Bristol which obviously was not it's original location. St. Mary Redcliff is no ordinary parish church, but one of the masterpieces of English Medieval architecture and is only a short distance from the site of several of the Bristol potteries.
The Bristol Museum has a very fine polychrome tile picture painted with a vase of flowers, birds and butterflies within an elaborate "Bianco-sopra-bianco" border (illustrated in Ray, fig. 12). In its present form the panel is 4 wide by 7 tiles high but was originally at least one row longer and was probably one of a pair. Delftware pieces painted with the thick "Bianco" decoration range in date from 1760-1768, and perhaps the closest parallels to this panel are the ship bowls dated 1764 and 1765 (Lipski, nos. 1194 and 1196). The odd fragments of a tile picture, no. **679** page 122, gives a glimpse of what was once made. These tiles were recovered from a Bristol house at the begining of this century. Unlike the other tile pictures in this catalogue, these tiles were not numbered on the reverse.

Fig. XXI. Two tiles from a blue Liverpool** tile picture, the reverse side having unusually elaborate markings. 12.6 x 0.7 cms. 1760-80.

Liverpool

A single large tile once existed showing "A West Prospect of Great Crosby 1716" and another lozenge shaped panel is known dated 1722 showing a coat of arms (Lipski, nos. 1691 and 1692) but there is no evidence to show that tile pictures were made in Liverpool before the second half of the 18th century. The largest surviving panel is in the Liverpool Museum (illustrated in "Fair as China Dishes"—Archer/Morgan, Pl. 78) which consist of 4 wide by 8 tiles high, painted with an elaborate shrub with flowers and birds decorated in "Fazackerly" colours. This picture was originally larger and had at one time formed a matching pair of panels, all the tiles being numbered on the reverse. The tile panel, no. **681** page 123, from the Bristol Museum is decorated in the same manner and is also a fragment of what had originally formed a matching pair of panels. Odd tiles from other Liverpool pictures occasionally turn up both in polychrome and blue and white, and all are clearly numbered on the back for easy assembly, see Fig. XXI.

The tile panels that have been discussed fall into two categories. Firstly, those made as trade signs whose intended use is quite clear, and secondly for decorative value. Panel no. **680** is clearly meant for a fireplace, but the larger pictures must have been placed in hallways, niches or conservatories. They are far too elaborate and expensive to be put into the pantry and were made to be seen, but unfortunately none have survived in situ.

Bristol/Liverpool

679. Part of a tile picture. Bristol.** 1755-75. Recovered from a house in Captain Carey's Lane, Bristol in 1904.
Each tile approx. 12.8 x 7.5 cms. (Reproduced by kind permission of Bristol Museum & Art Gallery).
The rather elongated house often appears on Bristol delftware, see fig. VI page 35, and (Britton, pp. 279, 280, 281) also compare the colouring of the trees with tile no. **318** on page 59. Unlike the illustrated London and Liverpool panels these tiles are not numbered on the back.

680. One of a pair of panels painted with exotic flowers and birds. Liverpool.** 1770-90. Each tile 12.9 x 0.6 cms.
Unlike no. **681** this pair of panels were made for a fireplace (the other half being a mirror image of the one illustrated). The tiles are numbered on the back in green (from the top row: 14-13, then: 12-11 etc.) which shows that the panels were only two across and that there were two more rows at the bottom and probably another row at the top. The tiles are thin and evenly made. This, and the use of green numbers on the reverse suggests a late date (no. 8 is a replacement).

681. 24 Tiles originally from a larger pair of panels.
Liverpool.** Circa 1760-80. Each tile approximately 13.1 x 0.7 cms. (Reproduced by kind permission of Bristol Museum & Art Gallery) (No. N5397.8).
The museum has 15 odd additional tiles and the numbering on their backs show that the picture has once formed part of a larger pair of panels. A similar "pair" are now in the Liverpool Museum, (illustrated in "Fair as China Dishes", no. 78).

LIVERPOOL PRINTED TILES

John Sadler was born in 1720 and was the son of a printer. He set up his own printing works in Harrington Street, Liverpool in 1748, but in 1757 gave up much of this business to concentrate on decorating tinglazed tiles.
Printing on ceramics seems to have been discovered in the 1740's although it remains uncertain as to whether John Sadler or a certain John Brooks (E.C.C. Trans. 1966 Vol. 9 Part 2) invented this technique, or that they were using other persons' discoveries. However the earliest transfer printed wares produced in any quantity were made by Sadler in August 1756. He acquired blank tiles from local potteries and decorated these with prints taken from woodblocks. A document in the Liverpool Museum confirms this early date:

"I, John Sadler, of Liverpoole, in the county of Lancaster, printer, and Guy Green of Liverpoole aforesaid, printer, severally make oath, that . . . they these deponents, . . . did within the space of six hours, . . . print upwards of twelve hundred earthenware tiles of different patterns, at Liverpoole aforesaid, and which, . . . were more in number, and better, and neater than one hundred skilful pot painters could have painted in the like space of time . . . and these deponents say they have been upwards of seven years in finding out the method of printing tiles . . .
John Sadler
Guy Green" (2nd August 1756)

David Drakard has very kindly supplied the following information on the techniques used by Sadler when transfer printing on tiles and creamware.
Research has produced evidence both physical and documentary that point to the use of the glue bat method of transfer. This very simple hand process for on-glaze printing required neither heat nor a printing press. The transfer medium was formed by pouring into flat pans warm, liquid, gelatinous animal glue, which on cooling became firm but flexible, resilient sheets of jelly with some elasticity and about 3mm. thick. To print, the copperplate was charged with a fine oil and cleaned off so that the oil was retained only in the engraving. A section of the glue jelly, cut to the size of the engraving to form the transfer bat, was pressed on the prepared copperplate. The flat, shiny surface of the bat picked up the minute quantities of oil from the engraving and, in turn, this was transferred by pressing the oily side of the bat onto the surface of the glazed ware. Colouring, in a fine powder form, was then dusted or pounced, as described in Sadler's notebook, over the oily impression with the surplus colour cleaned off and the ware was passed through the enamel kiln to fix the colour. At the end of the day the glue bats would be melted down and the process started all over again. Full descriptions of the technique are to be found in Josiah Wedgwood's "Common Place Book" of the mid 1780's and in Baker's patent for printing on glass of 1781.
Glue bat transfers will do what paper transfers cannot. They will stretch without tearing and thus can conform to the shape of ceramic wares without unsightly creases or rents. However this very stretch caused distortion of the print. Practical demonstration by Paul Holdway has shown that the prints on Sadler tiles taken from the same copper do not remain exactly the same shape, having slight varying distortions, a fault not occurring when tissue paper transfers are used, a medium that does not stretch to any degree before tearing. Furthermore, early Sadler prints sometimes show a typical fault of small unprinted blemishes caused by air or dirt with air trapped between the impervious bat and the surface of the ware. Such a fault does not occur with tissue paper transfers as trapped air passes through the wet paper during rubbing down. Distortion without tears and circular blemishes are certain indications of transfer by the glue bat method.

The long term financial rewards were obvious and with the introduction of this new process. Sadler claimed that, whereas a tile painter could decorate only two tiles an hour, he himself could print one hundred. (Compare the complicated Louis XV border, p. 44 with the printed examples on p. 126). The finished tiles were considerably neater and sold at half the price underselling the Dutch imports. Sadler exported large quantities of woodblock tiles to the New World some of which are still in situ in their original fireplaces ("John Sadler" Stanley Price, Pl. 2 and 3).
Sales were not the success that had been hoped for, and the early woodblock designs, (p. 126) were produced for only about six months.

From 1758 Sadler introduced printing from copper plates which resulted in a more detailed and clearer picture. Nearly all the tiles produced during 1758-61 had elaborate individual borders, the earlier ones being the more flamboyant with the colour of the scenes varying between pale lilac, red, brown, sepia and black.

Why some tiles are signed and others not, is a mystery. About 28 subjects have been recorded with a signature but most of these are also known without. The recorded signatures include "Sadler" by itself or sometimes with "Liverpool" or Liverp¹". Also 'J. Sadler" sometimes with the addition of "Liverpool" or "Liverp¹". All these signed tiles must be earlier than 1761 as this is the date when Guy Green was taken on as a partner. (One example is known of a tile signed with "Sadler C. Liverpool" which may be of later date.)

The pre-partnership designs continued to be made, although some of the signed examples have their signature partly removed cf. no. **712**. Stanley Price has suggested that Guy Green was taken on when Sadler undertook to print Wedgwood creamware. This seems plausible as the production line was soon to become overwhelmed with creamware orders, and tile production became relegated to second place. Few new designs were introduced during this period and the old patterns were re-used, sometimes re-cutting the copper plates when they became worn, cf. nos. **713** and **714.**

After 1765 many new designs were introduced; these being usually surrounded by a simple border known as the "88" due to the double loop at each side. These later tiles were predominantly printed in black and sometimes red. They are also known in sepia, brown, purple and there is even a turquoise green example in the Preston Museum of "The Lark and her young ones".

Guy Green continued to run the business after Sadler retired in 1770. Only one tile design is known, no. **723,** that includes the signature "Green" but it is assumed that he introduced other new scenes including the popular Aesop's Fables series (p. 131) of which there are 45 different recorded subjects. All of these have the 88 border barring one which for some reason has a square frame inside the border, (no. **731**).

The well known theatrical series of printed tiles were produced mainly in black but sometimes red (p. 133). They can be fairly closely dated as most of the designs have been taken from such publications as Bell's "British Theatre and Shakespeare" 1776-77, and Lownde's "New English Theatre" of 1775. (Fig. XXII, p. 133).

Tiles printed in black with a green wash and showing neo-classical scenes (p. 132) were the height of fashion during the last quarter of the 18th century. The designs were inspired by Wedgwood, those with the white ground costing 4/- per dozen (no. **734**) and those with the green ground, 4/6 per dozen (no. **733**).

On 10th December 1773 Richard Abbey announced in the Liverpool Advertiser that he was manufacturing all sorts of printed wares which included tiles. Abbey had had an apprenticeship with Sadler and Green and was therefore well versed with the techniques of printing on ceramics. Only one tile is known which is signed "Abbey Liverpool", this being one of a distinctive group of theatrical tiles (cf. no. **753**) although his name does appear on other printed ceramics. It has also been suggested that he may have made the green urn tiles (nos. **738-739**) as their simple border is similar to his theatrical tiles, although this has not been proven.

Very few printed tiles remain in situ in fireplaces in this country. Probably the best examples are at Croft Castle in Herefordshire which was refurbished in the 1760's. A large number of tiles were exported to the New World where they were used in fireplaces, a number of which remain intact today, (cf. "John Sadler"—Stanley Price). ("Sadler Tiles in Colonial America"—Bridges, E.C.C. Vol. 10, Part 3, 1978).

Most of the printed designs have been recorded by Anthony Ray and have been published in E.C.C. Vol. 9, Part 1 1973. Other subjects have since appeared and have been published subsequently.

E.C.C. Vol. 10 Part 1, 1979 Page 79.
E.C.C. Vol. 10 Part 3, 1978 "Sadler Tiles in Colonial America"—Bridges.
E.C.C. Vol. 11 Part 1, 1981 Page 36.
E.C.C. Vol. 11 Part 2, 1982 Plate 80.
E.C.C. Vol. 13 Part 2, 1988 Page 152.

All the tiles illustrated here have been given Ray's E.C.C. reference numbers which appears in brackets after the subject description except for nos. **686** and **753**, which had previously been unrecorded.

Liverpool

WOODBLOCK PRINTED TILES 1756-7

This was the earliest process which did not last more than about 6 months.

682. 12.7 x 0.7 cms. A scene from a novel or play (A3-1). A version printed in blue is in the British Museum.

683. 12.8 x 0.7 cms. Canal Scene in Holland (A5-3).

684. 12.7 x 0.8 cms. A girl at a table accompanied by a man smoking (A1-3). This example is different from the one illustrated by Ray having an extra "inner border" of circles.

685. 12.7 x 0.8 cms. A Gallant kissing a girl's hand perched on rocaille (A1-4). Taken from a design by Johann Esaies Nilson's "Coffee, Tea and Tobacco Ornament" (cf. E.C.C. Vol 9 Part 1, Pl. 30). Although a similar design to the previous, it has printed much clearer and sharper.

686. 12.7 x 0.7 cms. Man fishing in a river. This scene is unrecorded.

These three tiles all have the Louis XV border. Compare with the handpainted tiles on page 44.

687. 12.7 x 0.7 cms. Riverscape with domed building to the right and a man fishing (Appendix A5-8, E.C.C. Vol 11 Part 2, 1982, p. 180). Compare the Cherub border with the hand painted examples on tile nos. **187-188**.

688. 12.8 x 0.7 cms. Shepherd Lovers with a dog (A2-3) printed in brown and then enamelled over the top (cf. Ray, no. 612). For a copper plate version of this subject see no. **689**.
The over enamelling technique was also done at a slightly later date with copper plate transfers (cf. Ray, no. 672).

Liverpool

COPPER PLATE PRINTED TILES 1757-61

Sadler started printing from copper plates which gave a sharper, more detailed picture. The earlier tiles have more elaborate borders and are usually printed in black but sometimes in pale lilac, red, brown and sepia. Several of the subjects are signed, (see p. 125).

689. 12.8 x 0.5 cms. (Reproduced courtesy of Liverpool Museum). Shepherd lovers with a dog (B3-4).
This same subject was used on woodblock tiles no. **688** and has been adapted from Boucher's painting "Les Armoures Pastorales".

690. 12.8 x 0.6 cms. A Shepherd waking a sleeping Shepherdess (B3-1).
This design also appears on woodblock tiles (cf. A2-4).

691. 12.7 x 0.8 cms. A Gallant offering a Girl a bird's nest (B3-2).
The design was possibly taken from the John Bowles "Drawing Book".

692. 12.7 x 0.8 cms. "Mlle Carmargo dancing to pipe and drum" (B3-11).
Signed "J. Sadler Liverp^l". The scene is adapted from Laurent Cass' engraving of a picture in the Wallace Collection by Lancret.

693. 12.7 x 0.8 cms. "Shuttlecock and Battledore" (B4-9).
Signed "J. Sadler Liverpool". This scene was also used on a slightly later tile which was printed in black and enamelled in colours (C2-2).

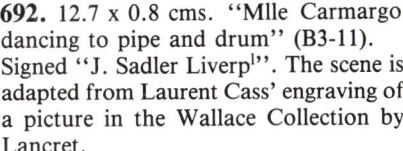

694. 12.6 x 0.8 cms. The Overturned Milk Pail (B6-3).
Signed "J. Sadler Liverp^l".

695. 12.9 x 0.8 cms. A Scholar teaching a girl to Sing (B6-5).
Signed "J. Sadler Liverp^l".

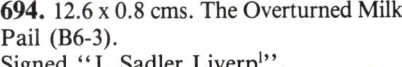

696. 12.7 x 0.7 cms. Children in fancy dress begging from street sellers (B5-1).

697. 12.7 x 0.7 cms. A Street Scene with a fiddler and a Girl dancing B5-2).
Signed "J. Sadler Liverpool".

Liverpool

1757-61

698. 12.7 x 0.7 cms. Black. The Sailor's Farewell (B6-20). There is another version of this subject (Ray, no. 678) which also appears on a printed delftware plate ("English Delftware"—Garner, Pl. 115B).

699. Black. The Sailor's Return (B6-21). The inn sign shows the King of Prussia, a popular subject for transfer prints on porcelain. The same subject was used on an earlier woodblock tile (A2-2) but with a different inn sign, the Lion of Scotland.

Quite often the tile subjects were produced as pairs.

700. 12.6 x 0.7 cms. Black. "The Tythe Pig" (B6-1). Taken from an engraving of 1751 by Muller after Boitard.

701. 12.8 x 0.7 cms. Black. Huntsmen and Peasant Couple with dead dog and bird (B6-2).

702. 12.8 x 0.7 cms. Black. A Gentleman putting on a Girl's skate (B3-12). Adapted from Larmessin's engraving of Lancret's "Winter".

703. 12.7 x 0.8 cms. Black. A Girl and a Pedlar resting under a tree (B6-17). Signed "J. Sadler Liverp¹".

704. 12.8 x 0.7 cms. Black. A Chinese Woman fishing accompanied by a boy (B7-1).

705. 12.7 x 0.7 cms. Black. Shepherd Lovers embracing (B3-6). Signed "Sadler Liverp¹".

1757-1770

706. 12.6 x 0.6 cms. Black. A Woman churning butter (B6-14). (Courtesy of Liverpool Museum).

707. 12.8 x 0.7 cms. Black. A Peasant having a tooth extracted (B6-18).

708. 12.7 x 0.7 cms. Black. A ruined portico and a bridge and tower on a river (B8-1). Signed "J. Sadler Liverpool".

The design for **706** has been taken from John Bowles' "Drawing Book" of 1756-7. The same figure also appears on a painted tile no. **198**.

No. **707** has been taken from an engraving by Jan Both after Andries Both and represents "Feeling", one of the five senses ("Some Liverpool Printed Tiles"—Bernard Watney, Burlington Magazine, May 1987).

709. 12.8 x 0.7 cms. Black. A Ship seen from the starboard bow (B9-2). Signed "Sadler Liverpool".

710. 12.7 x 0.7 cms. A ship from the starboard quarter with jib set (B9-7). Black. (Courtesy of Liverpool Museum).

711. 12.4 x 0.7 cms. (approx). A pilot cutter and a schooner seen from the starboard bow (C1-6). Black. (Courtesy of Liverpool Museum).

No. **709** and **710** are two of nine recorded ship designs of this type.
No. **711** is one of a group of seven similar designs that are very detailed but printed faintly. These are rare and Ray has suggested that they are slightly later in date (1761-5?).

712. 12.7 x 0.6 cms. Black. A Gentleman helping a Girl over a stile (B4-2). Signed "Sadler".

713. 1757-61.
12.7 x 0.8 cms. Black. A Girl with a basket and a fortune teller with a baby on her back. (B6-9).

714. 1760-70.
12.7 x 0.7 cms. Black but a whiter ground. Same subject as previous tile.

The engraving of **712** predates the Sadler and Green partnership of 1761 although some attempt has been made to erase the signature, see notes on p. 125.

No. **714** is a later version of **713**, the block having been re-engraved with the addition of extra grasses, hatching on the wall, clouds, etc. Note the border is less sharp than on the earlier version. (See p. 125).

Liverpool

?1765-75

715. ?1765. 12.7 x 0.7 cms. Brown/Black. An overturned basket with birds, from the "Ladies Amusement", plate 74 [(Ray, E.C.C. Vol. 11 Part 2, Appendix p. 159 (B2-2)].

716. 12.8 x 0.7 cms. Red. Abraham and Isaac (D1-1).
No. **716** is one of only four religious subjects that have been recorded on printed tiles.

717. 12.8 x 0.7 cms. Black. The Little Marquis and his Valet. (D3-3).
The design for no. **717** is from a picture called "Le Petit Maitre et son Valet" by Brandoin.

During this period the "88" border became standard for new designs although no. **175** may be from the early period.

718. 12.7 x 0.7 cms. Black. A man offering a birdcage to a girl with a child (D5-7).

719. 12.7 x 0.7 cms. Black. A lady and gentleman by a gothick folly (D4-2).

720. 12.5 x 0.6 cms. Black. A gentleman doffing his hat to the ladies (D4-1).

No. **719** is adapted from a print by W. Woollett, June 1757, of the Duke of Argyll's garden at Whitton (E.C.C. Vol 9 Part 1, 1973, Plate 32B). The scene on **720** is taken from the "Ladies Amusement", Plate 28 and is also known on a fragment of a painted tile in the Liverpool Museum.

721. 12.7 x 0.6 cms. Black. The Turkish merchant (D61).

722. Circa 1775. 12.8 x 0.7 cms. Red. The Pretty Mantuamaker (D5-27).

723. Circa 1775. 12.9 x 0.7 cms. Black. Three Chinese figures with a letter from a "chinoiserie alphabet" (D6-3). Signed "GREEN". (Courtesy of Liverpool Museum).

The design for **721** is known on Wedgwood creamware. Note the variations on the "88" border which in this instance is more obvious. No. **722** is taken from a print by Grignion after Brandoin, published in 1772. No. **723** is the only design recorded with the signature "GREEN". The scene is taken from Pillement's "Petits Parasols Chinois" which was published in 1774.

Liverpool

1770-80

724. 12.6 x 0.7 cms. Black.
The Bear and the Beehive. (D8-3).

725. 12.5 x 0.7 cms. Black.
The Hunted Beaver (D8-4).

726. 12.7 x 0.7 cms. Black.
The Fox and the Crow. (D8-20).

727. 12.5 x 0.7 cms. Red.
The Lion and the Frog. (D8-32).

728. 12.9 x 0.7 cms. Black.
Mercury and the Woodman. (D8-34).

729. 12.7 x 0.7 cms. Red.
The Old Hound. (D8-35).

730. 12.5 x 0.6 cms. Black.
The Sow and the Wolf. (D8-39).

731. 12.6 x 0.7 cms. Black.
The Fowler and the Ring Dove. (D8-17).
This is the only Fable subject that occurs
with a different border.

732. 12.9 x 0.7 cms. Black.
The Two Travellers and the Bear.
(D8-42).

Forty-five Aesop's Fables designs have been recorded of which all occur in the Croxall's Edition. Some of these designs were used to decorate a set of creamware plates in the Schreiber Collection (Victoria and Albert Museum). Three of the subjects used being the same as **725, 728** and **729**.

Liverpool

NEO-CLASSICAL DESIGNS CIRCA 1775-80

733. 12.6 x 0.6 cms. Black with green ground. A Muse with a lyre. (E1-7a).

734. 12.6 x 0.6 cms. Black and green with white ground. Apollo. (E1-6).

735. 12.9 x 0.7 cms. Black with green ground. Fortune (E1-8).

These tiles were printed in black and enamelled in green. Those with a solid ground were more expensive than those without (p. 128). The designs were taken from engravings by J. S. Muller illustrating an edition of "Horace" published by William Sandby in 1749. Other subjects (not illustrated here) were inspired from classical objects and coins, and also directly copied from "Wedgwood and Bentley" plaques.

736. 12.7 x 0.6 cms. Black and Green. A covered urn with bull's head and swags. (E2-10).

737. 12.7 x 0.6 cms. Black and Green. A lozenge shaped vase with an acanthus scroll and a portrait medallion. (E2-14). Seventeen variations of classical urn with the heavy border have been recorded.

738. 12.7 x 0.6 cms. Black and Green. Urn with ram's head and swags (E3-4).

739. 12.7 x 0.6 cms. Black and Green. Ovoid urn with a mask and swags (E3-5). Ray has suggested that these tiles with the more simple border, of which seven designs are known were printed by Abbey on the grounds of their similarity to his theatrical tiles, cf. no. **753**.

740. 12.7 x 0.7 cms. Black and Green. Flowerhead (G1-1). Similar designs but with a different flower are in the Liverpool Museum and another variation of this is in the Victoria and Albert Museum.

741. 6.5 x 0.6 cms. Black, Green and Orange. Acanthus and Ribbon scroll (G2-3). Other border tiles are on page 70. Quarter width printed tiles are also known. (E.C.C. Vol. 9 Part 1, 1973 Pl. 60). (Courtesy of Liverpool Museum).

THEATRICAL SUBJECTS 1777-1780

These tiles can be closely dated as most of the subjects have been taken from Bell's "Shakespeare and British Theatre" and Lownde's "New English Theatre". See fig. XXII, page 134.

742. 12.4 x 0.8 cms. Black.
Mrs. Abbington in the character of Estifania (F1-1).
Taken from Bell's "British Theatre" dated 20th May 1776.

743. 12.7 x 0.7 cms. Black.
Mr. Garrick in the character of Abel Drugger (F1-8).
From Johnson's "The Druggist", the print is taken from Sayer's "Dramatic Characters" published in 1770.

744. 12.5 x 0.7 cms. Black.
Mrs. Hartley as Lady Jane Grey (F1-11).
Taken from Bell's "British Theatre" dated 26th December 1776.

745. 12.7 x 0.6 cms. Black.
Mrs. Hartley in the character of Imoinda (F1-12).
From Southern's "Oroonoko", taken from Bell's "British Theatre" dated 1st March 1777.

746. 12.5 x 0.8 cms. Black.
Mr. Lee Lewes in the character of Harlequin from "Harlequin's Invasion" (F1-17).
This is copied from an unknown print. Compare it with no. **749** for a different version of the same character. Mr. Moody as Joe Simon no. **750** is a character from the same play.

747. 12.7 x 0.7 cms. Black.
Mr. Lewis in the character of Douglas (F1-19).
From Holme's "Douglas", the actor is William Thomas Lewis. The print is taken from "New English Theatre" dated 21st June 1777.

748. 12.7 x 0.6 cms. Black.
Mr. Moody in the character of Teague (F1-25).
From Howard's "The Committee". The print is from Bell's "British Theatre" dated 1st July 1776.

749. 12.7 x 0.7 cms. Black.
Mr. Lee Lewes in the character of Harlequin from "Harlequin's Invasion" (F1-16).
Compare with no. **746**.

750. 12.4 x 0.7 cms. Black.
Mr. Moody as Simon in "Harlequin's Invasion" (F1-24).
Taken from a print published in 1769.

Liverpool

751. 12.9 x 0.7 cms. Black.
Mrs. Yates as Lady Townley (F1-35). In Vanbrugh's "The Provok'd Husband". Taken from the print shown in fig. XXII. (Reproduced by courtesy of Liverpool Museum).

752. 12.9 x 0.7 cms. Black.
Mr. Smith in the character of L^D. Townley (F1-27).
Taken from the same play, see fig. XXII. (Reproduced by courtesy of Liverpool Museum).

Fig. XXII. Mr. Smith and Mrs. Yates in the characters of Lord and Lady Townley published for Bell's "British Theatre" Nov. 24th 1776.
(Reproduced by courtesy of Liverpool Museum).

753. 12.7 x 0.7 cms. Black.
Mr. Wilson in the character of the MINER Act 4th Scene Last.
Printed by Richard Abbey. This is a previously unrecorded pattern. A tile in the Liverpool Museum with the same swag border design is signed "Abbey Liverpool".

BIBLIOGRAPHY

- MICHAEL ARCHER and BRIAN MORGAN—"Fair as China Dishes, English Delftware" (International Exhibitions Foundation 1977-79).
- FRANK BRITTON—"English Delftware in the Bristol Collection" (Sotheby Publications 1982).
- FRANK BRITTON—"London Delftware" (Horne 1987).
- ENGLISH CERAMIC CIRCLE TRANSACTIONS—Vol. 9 Part 1 1973
  Vol. 9 Part 2 1974
  Vol. 10 Part 1 1976
  Vol. 10 Part 3 1978
  Vol. 11 Part 1 1981
  Vol. 11 Part 2 1982
  Vol. 12 Part 1 1984
  Vol. 13 Part 2 1988
- F. H. GARNER and MICHAEL ARCHER—"English Delftware" (Faber & Faber 1948).
- JAMES HALL—"Hall's Dictionary of Subjects and Symbols in Art" (Murray 1974).
- JONATHAN HORNE—"A Catalogue of English Delftware Tiles" (Horne 1980).
- IVOR NOEL HUME—"Early English Delftware from London and Virginia" (Colonial Williamsburg Occasional Papers in Archaeology, Volume II).
- C. H. DE JONGE—"Dutch Tiles" (Praegar 1971).
- JOURNAL OF THE SOCIETY OF POST MEDIEVAL ARCHAEOLOGY—"Post Medieval Archaeology, Vol. 4 1970".
- JONATHAN KINGHORN and GERARD QUAIL—"Delftfield, A Glasgow Pottery" (Glasgow Museums and Art Gallery 1986).
- ARTHUR LANE—"A Guide to the Collection of Tiles" (Victoria and Albert Museum HMSO).
- HANS VAN LEMMEN—"Delftware Tiles" (Shire Publications, Album 179).
- LIPSKI and ARCHER—"Dated English Delftware" (Sotheby Publications 1984).
- ARNOLD PAGE—"English Delftware Tiles" (Abson Books 1975).
- PHILADELPHIA MUSEUM OF ART—"Dutch Tiles" (Philadelphia Museum of Art 1984).
- ANTHONY RAY—"English Delftware Tiles" (Faber & Faber 1973).
- ANTHONY RAY—"English Delftware Pottery in the Robert Hall Warren Collection, Ashmolean Museum, Oxford" (Faber 1966).

34625 A